From The Library
of
RUTH N WETTLAUFER

Search the Scriptures

Second and Enlarged Edition

ROBERT B. GREENBLATT, MD, CM

Medical College of Georgia

Search the Scriptures

MODERN MEDICINE AND BIBLICAL PERSONAGES

Second and Enlarged Edition

With an Introduction by
WALTER C. ALVAREZ, MD

and a Foreword by
RALPH McGILL, LL D

J. B. LIPPINCOTT COMPANY
Philadelphia & Toronto

COPYRIGHT © 1963, 1968 BY J. B. LIPPINCOTT COMPANY

This book is fully protected by copyright and, with the exception of brief abstracts for review, no part of it may be reproduced in any form without the written permission of the publisher.

First Edition: first printing, 1963; twelfth printing, 1967.
Second and Enlarged Edition: first printing, August, 1968.

Distributed in Great Britain by
Pitman Medical Publishing Company, Limited, London

Library of Congress Catalog Card No. 68-28869
PRINTED IN THE UNITED STATES OF AMERICA
SP-B

DEDICATED TO

The students of the Medical College of Georgia
Thirty classes of whom I have been
privileged to teach, to advise, to
direct and, some of them, to inspire,
and who dedicated to me their 1960
yearbook *The Aesculapian*

The College's distinguished President and past Presidents

HARRY B. O'REAR, MD

G. LOMBARD KELLY, MD   EDGAR R. PUND, MD

Each of them has supported the
Chair of Endocrinology

Introduction to the Second and Enlarged Edition

HERE IS A DELIGHTFUL BOOK and thought producing. The Bible is full of medical stories, stories of illnesses of many of the principal characters, of David, Absalom, and particularly Job. There are stories of epidemics and stories of epilepsy and leprosy, of barrenness in women and of the "coldness" in the aging David—coldness that could not be warmed. There are so many stories of interest to a physician—and to clergymen, and to all people who follow clergymen.

The important point is that a very able and well-read physician can throw much light on these medical stories. This Dr. Greenblatt has done, and has done in such a delightful way that thousands of people have found pleasure in reading the first edition of this book.

Some seventy-five years ago, Sir William Osler, greatest physician of his time, said that a physician ought to be well-educated not in the science of medicine alone but in many fields of literature. Dr. Greenblatt is that kind of doctor: not only a fine gynecologist and a fine endocrinologist, but a fine, friendly and well-informed man. His scriptural and medical correlatives are well chosen, witty, and full of understanding.

WALTER C. ALVAREZ, MD

Chicago, Illinois
29 July, 1968

Foreword to the First Edition

AS A PERSON who grew up in a Calvinist, Bible-reading family, and as one who has a continuing pleasure in reading the Bible and the various translations of it, and also the Talmud, I found myself absorbed and fascinated by Dr. Robert B. Greenblatt's *Search the Scriptures*.

While the Bible was not written as history, it does contain much history. The people of the new nation of Israel have used the Old Testament to discover old wells, the copper mines of Solomon, and other valuable findings. I will never forget an Israeli army commander telling me that in the war that produced the independence of Israel, it was his recollection of a battle tactic of Biblical days that helped him win a small, but important, engagement.

Now comes Dr. Greenblatt, an eminent physician and endocrinologist, to open new doors in the Bible. If poor health and physical afflictions motivate man today, they assuredly did in the days of the prophets. I am especially grateful, for example, to have a new version of Esau's problem. I long have felt that he somehow has had a bad deal and have been unwilling to believe that he acted out of gluttony. Also, after some forty years in the newspaper business, I am weary of politicians and of writers of letters-to-the-editor who repeat, ad nauseam, the charge that someone with whom they disagree "has sold out for a mess of pottage."

All of us have given too little attention to Esau's statement to Jacob: "Feed me with that same red pottage; for

I am faint: . . . Behold, I am at the point to die: and what profit shall this birthright do to me?"

Dr. Greenblatt, looking at this with a scientist's eyes, agrees with, and amplifies, an earlier suggestion that Esau was in a fainting state because of a condition known as *hypoglycemia,* the syndrome of low blood sugar. The pottage that Esau craved was of lentiles—and the relief for his weakness and black-out condition is protein such as lentiles provide. To this day, lack of protein is a health problem in the Middle East, as it was to Esau.

Each of the chapters discusses some Biblical personality, or psychological climate, from the scientific aspect. I unreservedly recommend *Search the Scriptures* as being rewarding beyond the highest expectation.

RALPH McGILL

Atlanta, Georgia
19 November, 1963

Preface to the Second and Enlarged Edition

THE MODERN PHYSICIAN'S approach to diagnosis permits a better understanding of some of the people of the Bible. Thus the concept, held historically, that Saul of Tarsus suffered from epilepsy can be sustained no longer. The "thorn in the flesh" that bothered the Apostle Paul throughout his life probably had psychosexual overtones, and was without relevance to the fainting spell on the road to Damascus. More in the perspective of present-day medicine is to view this episode not as a catatonic convulsion but rather as a collapse from heat prostration, caused by excessive sweating with salt depletion.

In the light of modern scientific knowledge, also, young David's conquest of the Giant of Gath is easier to understand. Because of a pituitary tumor pressing on the optic nerve, most giants have limited peripheral vision. Perhaps David, observing Goliath's clumsy head movements, approached him unafraid, realizing that his wisdom and courage must prevail. The ignominious defeat of the blustering giant underlined for all posterity that "the battle is not always to the strong."

A parallel is at hand in the six-day war between the two million Israelis and the forty million Arabs. Before hostilities began, Nasser boasted repeatedly that he would hurl the Israelis into the sea. Now that the armies of Egypt, Jordan, and Syria have been swiftly vanquished, "proclaim it not in Gath" that the secret weapon of Israel was, like David's, wisdom and courage.

Search the Scriptures

I hope that the clarification of many puzzling or sometimes confusing situations may bring the reader matter for thought and much increase his pleasure when searching the scriptures.

ROBERT B. GREENBLATT, MD, CM

Augusta, Georgia
29 July, 1968

Preface to the First Edition

IF YOU HAVE WONDERED what man is, what woman—the miracle of reproduction, growth and development; why some are tall and others short, some weak and others strong; how in our world's competitive bustle man copes with rage, hate, and the sweats of insecurity and apprehension, yet also loves and laughs and labors with joy —you may wish to *Search the Scriptures*, linking the Bible's very old with today's very new medicine, and learning somewhat of the human endocrines and of their work within us.

Born of quite other essays written at the behest of the students at the Medical College of Georgia, and then, as *A Physician's Quest*, privately published, *Search the Scriptures* connects the human with the scientific mode of medicine by examining some facets of Biblical medicine under the light of our latest scientific knowledge. It is the book not at all of a theologian, make sure, but of a physician and endocrinologist, who considers the Bible the world's greatest literary work, and who believes that the better informed we are of the past the wiser we are in the present and the humbler against the future.

Often, in my lectures over the past quarter-century, I compared Biblical disorders with today's endocrinopathies, psychologic happenstances with hormonal drive, or the probable ailment of one who changed the course of history with a current illness or syndrome. These analogies fascinated my students, avid for knowledge of the Bible, of other classics, and of history; they seemed to fill a need. "His studie was but litle on the bible" is common not alone to Chaucer's Physician, particularly as we now limit, in our public schools, the uses of the Bible and its drama of all humanity.

From *Search the Scriptures* emerges a lesser theme: the place of modern medicine and of today's physician. Recent advances in medicine, particularly in endocrinology, are wonders of the world. Only thirty years ago, pneumonia was a probable, adrenal gland failure (Addison's disease) a very possible, and surgical removal of the adrenals a certain death certificate. Today, persons with pneumonia are well, often within a few days, thanks to eight or ten capsules of penicillin or tetracycline, and persons with Addison's disease or without their adrenals have lived for more than two decades, thanks to cortisone.

Yet the status of the physician, always the peer of priests, judges, and scholars, may be lower than it was a half-century ago. The history of medicine is the history of humanity, Garrison has observed, with "its brave aspirations after truth and finality, its pathetic failures"; and perhaps the physician's place has risen and fallen with it. Perhaps too pessimistic, Job spoke of "physicians of no value"; and, perhaps erring with optimism, Stevenson wrote that "the physician almost as a rule" stood "above the common herd" and was, indeed, "the flower" of civilization.

I would express my gratitude to all who have written on medicine and to my teachers, students, and colleagues, whom space forbids me to name here. But I would thank, especially, Mr. Lawrence M. Lande, for his wise counsel; the Rev. Dr. Norman Goldburg, for his frequent and pleasant help; Mrs. Martha Bell for her research and Mrs. Violet Welch for her assistance; Mr. Ralph McGill, for the kindness of his Foreword; and Mr. Carter Harrison, of the J. B. Lippincott Company, for his learned editing and warm help, both beyond the call of duty.

ROBERT B. GREENBLATT, MD, CM

Augusta, Georgia
30 October 1963

Contents

CHAPTER		PAGE
Introduction, 1968		9
Preface, 1968		11
Preface, 1963		13
1	*The Way of a Maid With a Man*	17
	Tamar, the wicked woman of Proverbs, Delilah, and Mary Magdalene	
2	*Conception and Contraception*	22
	Onan, Tamar, and Today's Contraception	
3	*Mandrake Root*	28
	Reuben's mandrakes, Rachel, and Leah	
4	*Behold, There Were Twins*	32
	The tools of science and Multiple births	
5	*Giants in Those Days*	37
	Goliath of Gath and the swordless David	
6	*Great of Will and Small of Stature*	42
	Zaccheus and the sycomore tree	
7	*Righteous Indignation*	47
	Joseph and Potiphar's wife	
8	*And They Sang Like Cherubs*	51
	Eunuchoidism and the castrati	
9	*Testament, Testimonial, and Testicle*	58
	Oath-taking and the genitals related	
10	*Token of the Covenant*	63
	Circumcision, circumvention, circumspection	
11	*At the Point to Die*	67
	Esau and his birthright	
12	*A Little Bit of Salt*	72
	Saul of Tarsus: Paul the Apostle	

Search the Scriptures

CHAPTER		PAGE
13	*Signs and Symbols*	78
	Symbols that tie man's times together	
14	*Seven and Seven*	84
	What is the symbolism of seven and of fourteen?	
15	*A Little Wine*	88
	For the weal or woe of mankind?	
16	*Give Yourself to Fasting*	98
	Effects harmful and beneficial	
17	*Fallen Angel*	102
	What is man?	
18	*A Vessel Full of Vinegar*	108
	Why has "vinegar" an unpleasant connotation?	
19	*Woman's Destiny*	113
	Puberty, reproduction, climacteric	
20	*A Woman's Garment*	118
	Cross-dressing and transvestism	
21	*Sins Be As Scarlet*	124
	Why are sins scarlet?	
22	*No Breasts Hath She*	129
	The "little sister" of Solomon's Song	
23	*Thy Faith Can Make Thee Whole*	134
	The woman having an issue of blood	
24	*When Desire Shall Fail*	138
	David, Abishag, and Bath-Sheba	
25	*Seven Ages*	143
	Man's aging and society's attitude	
26	*Hewers of Flesh and Drawers of Water*	150
	"The skill of the physician shall lift up his head." Whither Medicine?	
	Glossary of Some Medical Terms	161
	Index of Names	165

1

The Way of a Maid With a Man

There be three things which are too wonderful for me, yea, four which I know not:
The way of an eagle in the air; the way of a serpent upon a rock; the way of a ship in the midst of the sea; and the way of a man with a maid.   Proverbs 30:18-19

> *Who can fathom the subtlety, the why and the wherefore, the mystifying ways of a maid with a man?*

FOUR WOMEN of the Bible are worthy of our scrutiny. The first is Tamar, the crafty widow who had the courage to resolve her quest for motherhood; the second is the nameless wanton wicked woman of Proverbs, whose feet would not abide in her house as she sought her fill of love; the third is Delilah, the enchantress, who betrayed her lover for handfuls of silver; and the fourth is Mary Magdalene, the penitent sinner, who displayed a spiritual love that transcended the highest expression of physical passion.

The way of a man with a maid, despite the awe of Proverbs, is an open book. It is basic and physiologic, and wonderful for all men worthy of the name man. But the way of a maid with a man is frequently beyond comprehension. Whether born of necessity, of greed, of ambition, or of love, locked in the secret recesses of a woman's mind and body are an intuitiveness and an ingenuity that are all-pervading and that contrive to preserve the species. The trafficking in sex may take the form of subtle love, or it may serve as a means to an end.

One of the earliest sociological histories of a woman's ingenuity is recorded in Genesis, a successfully laid scheme for motherhood and marriage by Tamar, daughter-in-law of Judah. Her marriages to each of Judah's two sons ended tragically with their early deaths. One day, as Judah set off to shear his sheep, Tamar, impersonating a prostitute, settled by the wayside and awaited his passing.

When Judah saw her, he thought her to be an harlot; because she had covered her face.
And he turned unto her by the way, and said, Go to, I pray thee, let me come in unto thee; (for he knew not that she was his daughter in law.) And she said, What wilt thou give me, that thou mayest come in unto me?
And he said, I will send thee a kid from the flock. And she said, Wilt thou give me a pledge, till thou send it?
And he said, What pledge shall I give thee? And she said, Thy signet, and thy bracelets, and thy staff that is in thine hand. And he gave it her, and came in unto her, and she conceived by him.
Genesis 38:15-18

When Tamar's pregnancy became apparent after several months, she was accused of harlotry and her own father-in-law ordered her burned to death. But she presented him with his pledges—his signet, his bracelets, and his staff; and Judah, surprised, acknowledged his ownership, absolved Tamar of guilt, saying "She is more righteous than I," and married her. Soon afterwards she gave birth to twins.

By way of a well-laid and craftily executed plan, Tamar won her man. Was this prostitution? Nay. It was a tender trap for an honored and respected personage and widower. Through levirate law, Tamar gained motherhood, a husband, and the continuation of her rights. (The laws of the levirate marriage—Deuteronomy 25:5-10—provided that a brother of a deceased man should, under certain circumstances, marry the widow.) Whether this be love, physical fulfillment, or attainment of security, it matters not. It was *un fait accompli* under the laws and customs of her time. Tamar attained her goal by exploiting her resources.

The Way of a Maid With a Man

For some women, sexual congress is merely a game—the chase and the kill, the satisfaction that attends the conquest of a man and his subordination to their will. They seek premarital or extramarital sexual relations not for profit but for pleasures, fancied or real. Their boredom and frustration are the root of their troubles. All too frequently, their disquietude is the product of a consuming ennui, temporarily interrupted by another adventure in sex, another conquest.

Proverbs provides us such a woman (7:9-13, 17-19):

In the twilight, in the evening, in the black and dark night:
And behold, there met him a woman with the attire of an harlot, and subtile of heart.
(She is loud and stubborn; her feet abide not in her house:
Now is she without, now in the streets, and lieth in wait at every corner.)
So she caught him, and kissed him, and with an impudent face said unto him, . . .
I have perfumed my bed with myrrh, aloes, and cinnamon.
Come, let us take our fill of love until the morning: let us solace ourselves with loves.
For the goodman is not at home, he is gone a long journey.

Across the past twenty-five centuries, this scene has not altered much. Now, as then, many a so-called good wife searches for another sexual experience while her husband is away. Is she a prostitute? Not really. Yet she often is more alluring and far more dangerous than the despised prostitute, who practices her art and trade for gain. Today, the incidence of venereal disease is rising seriously, and its rise is caused more by promiscuity than by prostitution. The warning sounded in Proverbs applies still. Beware! "For she hath cast down many wounded . . ." (7:26).

Acting from quite other motives was Delilah, temptress and seducer of the mighty Samson, whose story has inspired at least three great works of art: Milton's epical poetic drama, *Samson Agonistes,* in 1671; Handel's oratorio, *Samson*, in 1743; and Saint-Saens' opera, *Samson et Dalila*, in 1877. Although a giant in strength, Samson became an easy prey in Delilah's arms. Her tender love was a snare; while she delighted him with her body's charms, she plotted to destroy him. For the lords of the Philistines, in order that they might slay Samson, had engaged her to discover the secret of his great strength. This she did, had his hair cut off, and reduced him to a man of ordinary strength whom her compatriots could capture and imprison —until his hair grew again and, "eyeless in Gaza," he brought down the temple on his enemies.

Was this prostitution? Was it not, in reality, big business, artful manipulation, and even patriotism, possibly? Delilah's reward was from "every one of us eleven hundred pieces of silver"—and, for a time, peace in her country.

Thence, we come to one of the most stirring narratives in the New Testament, that of a woman who had fallen from grace and regained it. Mary of Magdala may well have suffered from a compulsion neurosis known as *nymphomania*. For was she not healed of her evil spirits and infirmities when Jesus cast out of her seven devils? Mary was a woman of rank and means; how else could she afford the expensive alabaster box of ointment which she brought to anoint the feet of Jesus?

And, behold, a woman in the city, which was a sinner, when she knew that Jesus sat at meat in the Pharisee's house, brought an alabaster box of ointment.
And stood at his feet behind him weeping, and began to wash his feet with tears, and did wipe them with the hairs of her head, and kissed his feet, and anointed them with the ointment.   Luke 7:37-38

Mary Magdalene became His truly faithful servant, for Jesus had transformed her life. A living example of humility and unselfish devotion, she displayed a love that was triumphant, no longer sensual but spiritual. Jesus said of her: "Her sins, which are many, are forgiven; for she loved much...." (Luke 7:47).

The Way of a Maid With a Man

Prostitutes have exemplified the essence of kindness and compassion. I am reminded of the English poet who, sick, alone, and destitute, was taken into the house of a kindly street-walker. He shared her bed; she fed and nurtured him back to health. Although the term Magdalene is defined by the Concise Oxford Dictionary as "reformed prostitute," in a world where cruelty and avarice, selfishness and hypocrisy run rampant, Magdalene has come to imply humility and lovingkindness, not a wayward woman.

The way of a man with a maid is not nearly so puzzling as the way of a maid with a man. Sexual behavior is a fabric of complexly woven threads: psychogenic, anatomic, philosophic, hormonal and state-of-health. Most men are easily aroused sexually; most women accept or reject passively. The frigid female refuses to accept a subordinate position to the stronger sex, and does not enjoy marital relations. The nymphomaniac has an insatiable sex drive; she constantly pursues gratification, however elusive and fleeting. An overwhelming sexual urge in other women is the expression of either an overabundance of certain hormones, whether endogenous or exogenous, or extreme end-organ sensitivity. But nymphomania is a *psychoneurosis,* manifested by a frenetic and unreasonable sexual drive.

One must remember, as he examines the physiologic and psychologic bases of sexual behavior, that sex may be only casually related to reproduction. To pry into the modus operandi of woman's every sexual reaction, from the deeply drawn breath to the total orgasm, is fraught with obstacles; yet to understand the sexual act is not to demean ourselves, for sex colors, in some degree, our entire lives. Unlike animals, men and women employ sex to attack, to defend, to preserve; and, happily, they sublimate their sexual behavior and modify it by way of their learning, experience, and culture. For most of us, it is well to remember His admonition (John 8:7), "He that is without sin among you, let him first cast a stone at her."

2

Conception and Contraception

Defraud ye not one the other, except it be with consent for a time, that ye may give yourselves to fasting and prayer; and come together again, that Satan tempt you not for your incontinency.   I Corinthians 7:5

> *Is temporary abstinence a satisfactory approach to contraception in love and marriage? How can man harness the "creative force" to avoid the world catastrophe of the population explosion?*

A THEME in the affairs of man pervading every civilization is that conjugal love should not be hampered by fear of conception of an unwanted child. Early in Genesis (38:9), we find the story of Onan, who spilled his seed on the ground. The Bible records Tamar's widowhood and the obligation of the younger brother to marry her according to levirate law. Onan was forced to marry Tamar but wished to avoid the entanglements of paternity. "Coitus interruptus," a primitive and elementary form of contraception, still is practiced widely. It is a practice that weighs on the conscience of man, and does violence to an act that should engender tenderness, fulfillment and the sublimest of emotional nuances. A great deal of illness among women, manifested in a dozen different ways, may be traced to such and other unsatisfactory sexual experiences.

Contraceptive techniques have been employed since ancient times. In the Egypt of old, a medicated tampon, prepared from a mixture of the tips of acacia shrub and honey, was inserted into the vagina. The remarkable feature of this recipe is that, under fermentation, acacia breaks down into lactic acid—one of the active spermicidal agents used today in the manufacture of contraceptive jellies. In the Dark Ages, Islamic women were advised to insert the flowers and seeds of cabbages into the vagina.

Various mechanical barriers have come into vogue from time to time. Along with sheaths, diaphragms and jellies, there have been gold collar buttons for insertion into the cervical os. The lowly camel driver, aware that his transportation system might break down should one of his camels become pregnant, prevented their conception by inserting a pebble into the uterine cavity. In the 1920's, Berlin's Ernst Graffenberg, now residing in Israel, transmuted the Arab camel stone into a ring of surgical silk or silver, gentle enough for the human womb. This was in preantibiotic days, and the use of the ring fell into disrepute, as much from the enmity of his professional colleagues as from corrosion, irritation and infections. But in recent years, the idea has been revised, and devices made of plastic have come into use again.

The intrauterine contraceptive device, known as the IUCD, may find its greatest use in countries where literacy is low and the population explosion dangerously high. Expulsion of the device, uterine bleeding, and cramps and discomfort occur in 10 to 15 per cent of the users, and the pregnancy rates vary from 1.1 to 6 per cent.

The rhythm method—that is, abstinence during the fertile period of a woman's cycle—is a method condoned, even encouraged, by the Roman Catholic Church. Not until 1930 did the Vatican modify the Augustinian rule that sex must be for procreation alone; then Pope Pius XI approved the rhythm method. A mandate for temporary abstinence, it would appear, is apparent in the Apostle Paul's Epistle to the Corinthians (1:7, 5).

Search the Scriptures

It has been conjectured that the rhythm method—discovered in this century as a method of limiting the family—was not new but merely a reaffirmation of what Paul had advised. Many years before the time of Paul, the Preacher (Ecclesiastes 3:2-5) spoke of "A time to be born, and a time to die; . . . time to embrace, and a time to refrain from embracing." To read into this passage some contraceptive plan is to reach beyond the realms of reason. The rhythm method—according to Dr. Edward Tyler, an eminent authority on planned parenthood—is only 75 per cent effective. Because of its relatively low efficacy, many conscientious women, who have tried rhythm and failed, have given the method the sobriquet of "Roman roulette." Claire Booth Luce, a prominent Catholic, has expressed the view that the rhythm method's calculated watching is tantamount to love according to plan. Nonetheless, it is still the only technique available to millions of practicing Catholics. When in 1954 Pope Pius XII made the statement that it was the responsibility of each family not to have more children than it could take good care of, he, in effect, struck a blow for birth control. Thus he joined the responsible leaders throughout the civilized world, who realize the ominous implications of the population curve.

The modern advances in contraception are the result of newer knowledge in hormonal physiology and the science of endocrinology. The study of endocrinology has revealed the mechanisms involved in ovulation and menstruation. Now that we have discovered these secrets, and pharmaceutical laboratories have synthesized the very hormones produced by the ovary (and many other steroid preparations that simulate the action of these hormones), we can utilize our knowledge to the betterment of mankind. We have harnessed these hormones so that we can imitate the menstrual cycle; we can reproduce some of the hormonal changes that take place early in pregnancy.

Soon after conception, the ovary produces hormones to

support the developing embryo and, at the same time, to prevent further ovulation, so that a woman will not conceive during her pregnancy. Nature has shown us the way, and we have applied these principles in the management of family planning. We have learned not only how to suppress ovulation but how to delay, as well as to advance, the onset of menstruation and to arrest excessive menstrual bleeding. We can help so to mould the woman of today that premenstrual tension, with all its attending unhappy situations, may be measurably lessened. We can postpone the menopause indefinitely, so that a woman in the autumn of her years need not suffer a winter of discontent. The "pill" offers women in the middle years a double blessing: through its use, the fears of childbirth are eliminated and the anxieties and depressions brought on by an impending menopause are minimized.

Now we have two methods of oral contraception, the conventional "combined" form and the "sequential." Each has certain desirable features, certain advantages. At least the physician *and* the patient have choices. Furthermore, the "pill" has many uses—to regulate the cycle, to ameliorate dysmenorrhea, to prevent incapacitating ovulatory pain (*mittelschmerz*), to mitigate severe premenstrual tension, to lessen unwanted hairiness and acne in the adolescent girl, and to treat the premenopausal and menopausal woman. The "pill" is virtually 100 per cent effective when properly taken—but there are few things *100 per cent* safe. Of course, complete continence is the only method 100 per cent sure to control birth—despite the recent claims of two Englishwomen that their conceptions were parthenogenetic. A London newspaper scornfully challenged their claims. One of the offended women, claiming that her virtue and good name were sullied, brought a suit in the Courts of Law. And the Courts awarded her damages of several thousand pounds.

The ultimate goal of contraceptive measures is to provide the means whereby the destiny of man and the welfare of our world are not left to chance sexual desire alone. War, famine, poverty are the spoiled fruits of overpopulation. Hitler's *drang noch osten*, his drive to the East, was as much for *Lebensraum* for his Germans as it was for conquest. His ambition was to acquire not only living room but the wheat fields of the Ukraine to feed the increasing Teutonic masses. Even laboratory rats, packed too many in one cage, become socially maladjusted and soon will devour one another.

In 1887, when the lines by Emma Lazarus were inscribed on the pedestal of the Statue of Liberty, the population of the United States of America was about 60 million, against today's more than 200 million.

THE NEW COLOSSUS

Not like the brazen giant of Greek fame,
With conquering limbs astride from land to land;
Here at our sea-washed, sunset gates shall stand
A mighty woman with a torch, whose flame
Is the imprisoned lightning, and her name
Mother of Exiles. From her beacon-hand
Glows world-wide welcome; her mild eyes command
The air-bridged harbor that twin cities frame.
"Keep ancient lands, your storied pomp!" cries she
With silent lips. "Give me your tired, your poor.
Your huddled masses yearning to breathe free.
The wretched refuse of your teeming shore.
Send these, the homeless, tempest-tost to me,
I lift my lamp beside the golden door!"

Today the United States can no longer extend this generous offer. It must instead decrease sharply the supplies of wheat and foodstuffs to the underprivileged, overpopulated countries of the world. Our wheat bins are being rapidly emptied—our population is soaring. Demographers estimate a US population of 500 million by 2015 —less than half a century off. Will the US suffer the fate of another India, of another China?

Whether or not the church plays a constructive role in

planned parenthood depends, according to sociologist Charles Hendry, on whether religious institutions are used to suppress or to release man's capacity to exercise moral responsibility. Reinhold Niebuhr believes that the function of religion is to help people develop and maintain basic faith in the meaning of life, in man's dignity, infinite worth and destiny. I have long felt that if the rhythm method is employed to circumvent conception, how can it differ morally from the pill or other contraceptive devices? The intent is the same, God is not deceived. Whatever methods are used for family spacing and limitation of the population explosion are also good for the family unit, the existing children, the health of a future child, and of the mother-wife. God is on the side of man. Every child should be wanted, planned, with a design for his future welfare—not just born, like sheep or goats. All of us are born *inter feces et urinam;* unfortunately far too many remain not far from the *feces* and the *urine.*

3

Mandrake Root

> And Reuben went in the days of wheat harvest, and found mandrakes in the field, and brought them unto his mother Leah. Then Rachel said to Leah, Give me, I pray thee, of thy son's mandrakes.
>
> And she said unto her, Is it a small matter that thou hast taken my husband? and wouldest thou take away my son's mandrakes also? And Rachel said, Therefore he shall lie with thee tonight for thy son's mandrakes. Genesis 30:14-15

Did Reuben's mandrakes have medicinal value for the promotion of fertility?

THE STORY OF JACOB'S MARRIAGE to his first cousins Rachel and Leah is a story of racial origins, of fertility and infertility, and of a bitter rivalry between two sisters.

After serving his uncle Laban for seven years, you will remember, in order to wed his younger daughter Rachel, "beautiful and well-favoured," Jacob discovered himself tricked; he was wedded to the firstborn daughter Leah, the "tender-eyed." So he took Rachel to wife also, promising to serve Laban "yet seven other years" for her, and loved her more than he loved Leah. Yet for a time Leah prevailed, because she could bear children. "And when the Lord saw that Leah was hated, he opened her womb": and she bore Jacob their firstborn son Reuben, him of the mandrakes, and three others, then "left bearing" until after the episode of the mandrakes.

Rachel's anguish because of her sterility bordered on the psychotic:

Mandrake Root

And when Rachel saw that she bare Jacob no children, Rachel envied her sister; and said unto Jacob, Give me children, or else I die.

And Jacob's anger was kindled against Rachel: and he said, Am I in God's stead, who hath withheld from thee the fruit of thy womb?   Genesis 30:1-2

So Rachel sent her maid Bilhah in unto Jacob, and she bore him two sons. And, countering, Leah sent her maid Zilpah in unto her husband, and Zilpah bore him two sons, also.

This, then, is the setting for Rachel's deal with Leah: Rachel would get Reuben's mandrakes, Leah would get the night with Jacob. Both agreed to the bargain, and it seems to have worked for both of them. For Leah now bore to Jacob two more sons and a daughter, and Rachel bore the son Joseph.

What role did the mandrakes play in overcoming Rachel's infertility, and perhaps Leah's, also? The mandrake, *Mandragora officinarum*, often mis-called Mayapple and Devil's apple, is a plant, growing in Egypt and Palestine, that is the source of a strong narcotic and of perhaps more superstitions than any other plant. Its long and twisted root, which resembles roughly the human form, was credited with many powers: to bring sleep, to kill pain, to increase wealth, to arouse ardor, to overcome barrenness. And on being uprooted, it was said to make such horrid screamings that to all who heard them came madness if not death.

Mandrakes and mandragora were known in medicine and in literature. In her dying speech, Juliet recalls the horror of the uprooted mandrakes (*Romeo and Juliet*, IV, 3):

> ... what with loathsome smells,
> And shrieks likes mandrakes' torn out of the earth,
> That living mortals, hearing them, run mad.

In the first century, the Greek physician Dioscorides described the use of mandragora wine in surgical anesthesia and in cauterizing wounds, listed it as a bringer of sleep—

"but being too much drank it drives out ye life"—and, following other physicians, classified it as an aphrodisiac. Mandrakes bear a gross resemblance to Mexican yams, which, rich in lipids, are today the chief source of materials for the commercial synthesis of sex-steroids. Growing wild in the Holy Land in the time of Rachel and Leah, long before Dioscorides, mandragora was believed to promote fertility.

The "Song" of John Donne (1573-1631), the "infidel in love" and Dean of St. Paul's, plays on this belief:

> Goe, and catche a falling starre,
>   Get with child a mandrake roote,
> Tell me, where all past yeares are,
>   Or who cleft the Divels foot,
> Teach me to heare Mermàides singing,
>   Or to keep off envies stinging,
>   And finde
>   What winde
> Serves to advance an honest minde.

But we have open to us a more plausible explanation of the role of the mandrakes in causing Rachel's fertility. From the earliest to the most recent times, a brew of the mandrake was used to quiet anxiety and to lull into rest and sleep those who sipped it. When Antony is returned to Rome in *Antony and Cleopatra* (I, 5), Cleopatra commands her servant:

> Give me to drink mandragora.
>   Why, madam?
> That I might sleep out this great gap of time
> My Antony is away.

And in *Othello* (III, 3), about to "lose" Desdamona's handkerchief in Cassio's lodging further to poison the mind of the approaching Othello, Iago gloats:

>   Not poppy, nor mandragora,
> Nor all the drowsy syrups of the world
> Shall ever medicine thee to that sweet sleep
> Which thou ow'dst yesterday.

Mandrake Root

The importance of tranquility and equanimity in the management of all aspects of illness was rediscovered half a century before Shakespeare wrote about mandragora and "all the drowsy syrups of the world." Ambroise Paré (1510-1590), a volunteer field surgeon, rebelled against the redhot iron in the treatment of battle wounds. He appreciated calming influences for his patients—to quiet nerves, to promote sleep, and to alleviate pain. He thought he had not only to cure but to comfort the sick, the wounded, and the dying. Called to Flanders to treat the Duke d'Auret, who had suffered for months from a gunshot wound, Paré emphasized the importance of environment, of equanimity, and of repose in treatment. He had flowers placed in the Duke's sickroom, induced his sleep by simulated rain—"by making water run from some high place into a cauldron"—and, to lift his patient's spirits, had violins played at his bedside. Small wonder that this lowly barber-surgeon ultimately became the sixteenth century's greatest surgeon.

The lesson to be derived from the story of Rachel and the mandrakes is often overlooked. What helped Rachel to conceive was not the fertilizing but the tranquilizing properties of the mandrake; the mandrakes soothed her anxieties and diminished the self-reproach that she suffered because of her barrenness.

The use of tranquilizers in the management of barren but otherwise healthy couples was recently tested in a carefully controlled experiment. Dr. Lawrence Banks and his colleagues treated thirty women, classified as "no reason for infertility," with daily doses of tranquilizer for three months. If conception did not occur during this period, the wife was continued on the medication *with her husband:* when both husband and wife were treated, pregnancy was fifty per cent greater. Far too long has the need to soothe anxieties and to eliminate self-reproach of both the wife and the husband been neglected in the treatment of infertility. Success may be achieved often—to "get with child a mandrake root."

4

Behold, There Were Twins

And when her days to be delivered were fulfilled, behold, there were twins in her womb.   Genesis 25:24

> *Can the tools of science be used today to foil the laws of nature and of genetics, and to induce multiple births?*

THE GENETIC PHENOMENON of multiple births is not yet fully understood, and many argue the relative importance of heredity and environment. A role of environment in biology was furnished us by Jacob's contractual arrangement with his father-in-law, Laban. After removing all the speckled and spotted cattle from Laban's herds, Jacob was to receive all those that were born with these very same genetic characteristics. Accordingly, Jacob exposed striped rods to the constant view of the animals: "And the flocks conceived before the rods, and brought forth cattle ringstraked, speckled, and spotted" (Genesis 30:39).

Shakespere used this episode, one may recall, as several kinds of background in *The Merchant of Venice* (I, 3):

> *Shylock.* When Jacob graz'd his uncle Laban's sheep—
> This Jacob from our holy Abram was. . . .
>   *Antonio.* And what of him? Did he take interest?
>   *Shy.* No, not take int'rest, not, as you would say,
> Directly int'rest. Mark what Jacob did. . . .
> This was a way to thrive, and he was blest;
> And thrift is blessing, if men steal it not.

Behold, There Were Twins

Twins are mentioned but three times in the Bible, twice in the Old and once in the New Testament. The Bible's famous twins were Jacob and Esau (Genesis 25:24-26). The others were Pharez and Zarah (Genesis 38:27-30), the offspring of Tamar, who enticed her father-in-law, Judah, into a levirate marriage. The only twin mentioned in the New Testament is the Apostle Thomas, called Didymus (John 20:24); the Greek word for twin is *didymus*. In Acts 28:11, Paul obliquely refers to twins when he mentions that he had wintered in the isle whose sign was Castor and Pollux. The ancient Greeks wove many legends about the gigantic twins, Castor and Polydeuces (the latter called Pollux by the Romans), offspring of Leda's amours with her mortal husband and the god Zeus.

Multiple siblings, regarded by many primitive people as evil spirits, were generally put to death. But other societies considered twins as a sign of favor from the fertility gods. Twins were honored as possessors of supernatural powers. Romulus and Remus, the twins nurtured by a wolf, according to Roman legend, were the founders of Rome.

The strong and sometimes psychic attachment of twins and more often their bitter rivalry have been dealt with in drama and fiction. The rivalry between Jacob and Esau is well known. The Bible states "and the children struggled together within her" (Genesis 25:22), probably representing the earliest reference on record of sibling rivalry. In the case of Pharez and Zarah, there was the struggle for emergence.

> And it came to pass, when she travailed, that the one put out his hand: and the midwife took and bound upon his hand a scarlet thread, saying, This came out first.
> And it came to pass, as he drew back his hand, that, behold, his brother came out: and she said, How hast thou broken forth? this breach be upon thee: therefore his name was called Pharez.

And afterwards came out his brother, that had the scarlet thread on his hand: and his name was called Zarah (Genesis 38:28-30).

In countries today in which the right of primogeniture is observed, the claim of the first born to the father's title or estate could have enormous significance. Among the royal families in Europe, should twins be born, the right to succession could be in dispute unless the first born is officially identified. When twins are fathered by a king of the Kuanyama of South Africa, one of the babies is killed by the midwives. Dumas played upon the theme of the twin problem in his novel, *The Vicomte de Bragelonne*. He made use of the legend that France's "Man in the Iron Mask" was actually the twin brother of Louis XIV, whom the King sought to keep out of the way.

Human twins are born once in every 80 pregnancies, triplets once in 6,400, quadruplets once in 512,000, quintuplets once in about 41 million. But new fertility agents have wrought havoc with such statistics. The incidence of multiple births in women treated with these agents has increased tenfold. These agents are *a.* Clomid, a pituitary gonadotropic releasing agent, *b.* Pergonal, an extract from the urine of menopausal women rich in human pituitary gonadotropins, and *c.* gonadotropins, extracted from human pituitary glands.

Incidentally, the Pergonal available in today's pharmaceutical market is derived from a process developed by Dr. Pietro Donini of Rome; the source of its menopausal urine is a nunnery housing aged nuns. The first clinical trials with this "extract" were performed by Dr. Bruno Lunenfeld in Israel. So Pergonal is doubly blessed, bearing the stamp of both Rome and the Holy Land.

Most investigators believe that monozygotic twinning (identical twins) is not hereditary, and that it occurs randomly, at any time, at any age, and in any population. Dizogotic twinning (fraternal or unidentical twins) occurs so frequently in some families that geneticists are certain that the tendency is inherited, decreases in frequency from North to South, and is extremely rare in some populations. Some 40 years ago, a Frenchwoman living in Cleveland, Ohio, gave birth as follows: with her first husband, twins; with her second husband, twins and triplets; with the third, twins, triplets and quadruplets. In 15 pregnancies, she bore 42 children, of whom 20 were stillborn, six died young, and 16 survived. In recent years, there has been a rash of reports of quadruplets and quintuplets born to women after the administration of fertility-inducing agents and sometimes some months after terminating a course of birth control pills (this latter phenomenon has not been substantiated statistically). Dr. Carl Gemzell, of Stockholm, Sweden—noted for the treatment of infertile women with gonadotropic extracts from human pituitaries—reported the birth of twins, triplets, quadruplets, quintuplets and sextuplets in his series. Man's upper limit seems to be sextuplets, although there have been recent reports of septuplets and octuplets. A 16th century memorial plaque in Germany tells of the births of seven living infants, the last of whom survived 11 days, but the story's veracity is doubtful. Not to be doubted, however, is the birth of septuplets to a Boston woman, 23 years old, at St. Margaret's Hospital on October 1, 1966. The three boys and four girls were born four months prematurely and, therefore, never really had a chance to survive. The husband, a garbage collector, gained brief immortality; actually, no prowess belonged to him, for his wife had been treated with one of the fertility-inducing agents.

With a better understanding of the use of fertility agents, the incidence of multiple births in excess of twinning may be greatly reduced. Dr. A. Carl Crooke, of Birmingham, England, uses human gonadotropins in a single massive dose instead of daily doses over a period of eight days or more. The incidence of multiple births in his cases has decreased considerably in comparison to that of his colleagues'. With the use of Clomid, the nonsteroidal pill that stimulates the release of the patient's own gonadotropins, many multiple births have been reported. From the 1,450 pregnancies on record following the administration of Clomid, two sets of quintuplets have resulted, six sets of quadruplets, eight sets of triplets, and 113 sets of twins. At the Medical College of Georgia, where the use of Clomid for the treatment of the anovulatory infertile women originated, eight sets of twins have been born out of a total of 86 deliveries. One set was monozygotic and must be considered a random event; the other seven sets were dizygotic due to multiple ovulations. All but one set survived; they remain well and apparently in good health. With lowered dosages of Clomid, it may well be that the incidence of triplets and quadruplets and other multiple births may be kept in check.

Science has reached the point where it can create a physiologic environment to increase the chances of multiple births and thus to make hereditary and genetic factors secondary. What is most awesome is the power over life and death now residing in the physician-scientist because of the great advances in human biology.

5

Giants in Those Days

And there went out a champion out of the camp of the Philistines, named Goliath, of Gath, whose height was six cubits and a span.

And he had an helmet of brass upon his head, and he was armed with a coat of mail; and the weight of the coat was five thousand shekels of brass.

And the Philistine said, I defy the armies of Israel this day; give me a man, that we may fight together. . . .

And David said to Saul, Let no man's heart fail because of him; thy servant will go and fight with this Philistine.

So David prevailed over the Philistine with a sling and with a stone, and smote the Philistine, and slew him; but there was no sword in the hand of David.   1 Samuel 17:4-5, 10, 32, 50

> *How could an unarmed youth dare battle the well-armored giant, Goliath? What permitted him to accept the challenge—bravado, faith, or knowledge born of clinical observation?*

THE PROWESS of giants is legend. Their conquest by men of normal proportion is celebrated in song and story. Many of us are familiar with the tale of Hercules' triumph over Antaeus, son of Terra, invincible so long as his feet touched the earth. Children delight in the age-old tale of "Jack and the Beanstalk," simply because a boy was able to best a giant. Yet the story of Goliath and David holds deeper meaning, and appeals to young and old. The giant Goliath, whom the Bible records as ten feet tall, was slain by the gentle shepherd lad, David, after swaggering forth for forty days to taunt the Israelites in battle array. He challanged them to send forth their champion whom he would engage in mortal combat, to decide whether the Philistines or Israelites were the victors.

Goliath was a fearful figure, who shouted defiance and hurled insults at the enemy. Then the youthful David arrived on the field, with food and a message that his father wished delivered to his older sons. He could observe closely the boastful, threatening giant, who failed to impress him. Being both perceptive and courageous, David soon requested King Saul's permission to accept Goliath's challenge. When the king was unable to dissuade him, he offered the youth full battle regalia, but David decided to face his foe unencumbered.

> And he took his staff in his hand, and chose him five smooth stones out of the brook. . . ; and his sling was in his hand: and he drew near to the Philistine.   I Samuel 17:40

Discovering his young opponent, Goliath cursed him, enraged that an untrained boy was chosen to represent the Israelites. He swore to make quick shrift of the matter.

Did David's boldness border on youthful irresponsibility and impulsiveness? It is far more likely that his keen powers of observation disclosed Goliath's peculiar movements. David probably realized that his opponent was forced to turn his entire head in order to focus his full gaze on an object. Also, he probably found significance in the fact that such a man needed to be heavily armored and used the services of a smaller Philistine to carry a coat of mail. This gave additional protection. In modern terms, one might say that he suspected the loud-mouthed giant of being "all bark and no bite."

Perhaps David suspected what we know today: giants are prone to suffer from lateral blindness. Giantism is frequently caused by a tumor of the pituitary gland. As such tumors enlarge, they encroach on the inner fibers of the optic nerves and thus compromise the nerve supply to the retina. When this occurs, the victim suffers from "tunnel

Giants in Those Days

vision." His sight is clear in a direct line, but not peripherally. David, therefore, would step agilely to the side when he had drawn close enough to Goliath. Then, as his adversary hesitated, clumsily turning his head to bring back the youth within his limited field of vision, David took deadly aim with the sling shot and struck the lone spot unprotected by heavy armor. The blow on his forehead spelled defeat for the giant. Thus David won his victory by superior knowledge, skill, and agility, rather than by brute force.

Giants have intrigued mankind since the dawn of history. Yet little was known of them until late in the 19th century, when an interrelationship was established between the pituitary gland and a type of giantism known as *acromegaly*. Pierre Marie's classic description of this filled a page in the early annals of endocrinology, directing attention to the pituitary gland as a regulator of growth. Subsequently, it was demonstrated that acidophilic cell tumors of the pituitary are often associated with *acromegaly* and *acromegalic giantism*. In ancient days, giants often were regarded as semigods. Genesis records:

> There were giants in the earth in those days; and also after that, when the sons of God came in unto the daughters of men, and they bare children to them, the same became mighty men which were of old, men of renown.   Genesis 6:4

The biblical scribe also referred to giants encountered by the Israelites as they made their way to the Promised Land. We read of the King of Bashan whose name was Og, and it is stated that his bedstead was made of iron. To portray his size, it was written that this measured nine cubits in length, and was four cubits wide. He was mentioned as being the only remaining giant (Deuteronomy 3:11). Among the most graphic descriptions, however, were those spoken by the men sent by Moses to look over the Land of Canaan before it was claimed by the Israelites. They reported that although the land flowed "with milk and honey," they dared not invade it because the inhabitants were giants "and we were in our own sight as grasshoppers, and so we were in their sight" (Numbers 13:33). Yet at a later time, Joshua led them in winning this land.

Despite such accounts, the question remains: did actual giants really inhabit the earth in the remote past? Did men with giant-sized proportions live during a prehistoric period? Of course, dinosaurs and gigantic beasts roamed the earth then. Their skeletons and life-like replicas are exhibited by such museums as the Smithsonian Institution. However, anthropologic discoveries have yet to provide evidence that human giants have ever existed.

But we know now that excessive stature falls into three categories: the first is caused by an increased secretion of growth hormone from the pituitary gland; the second is hereditary, due to genetic factors; and the third results from continued linear growth when inactive gonadal hormones fail to stimulate closure of the epiphyses, the growing end of bones, and such victims are known as eunuchoidal giants. This third type, the eunuchoid, is generally beardless, weak, shy, nonaggressive, and his muscle mass is poor—the opposite of tall, agile, well-coordinated, and virile men of basketball fame, whose statures are the products of genetics and good nutrition. This type, found in certain areas of the world, includes the Watusis and Dinkas of Africa. Members of these tribes are famed for their excellent physiques: it is not unusual for them to exceed seven feet in height.

The height of young girls is increasing considerably. We now see adolescent girls who are 66 to 69 inches in height, with a potential of 72 inches and more. For those destined to be extremely tall, much may be done to curtail and limit the growth spurt that occurs between the ages of 11 and 13 years.

The administration of large continuous doses of estrogens (the female hormone) for six to 18 months, and the induction of menses with small courses of progestogen administered at monthly intervals, will hasten closure of the growing ends of the bones (epiphyses), so that the girls will reach a height of two to four inches less than that predicted by growth tables. It is now possible to mitigate the economic, psychological, and physical handicaps associated with excessive tallness in girls.

We are aware that an occasional circus freak is afflicted with pituitary giantism. Yet well-known personalities of our time may also have had this disorder. Primo Carnera, that towering prize fighter, had definite acromegalic features. The most unforgettable, however, was Luis Firpo, who challenged Jack Dempsey for the world's heavyweight boxing title. To everyone's astonishment, he knocked Dempsey through the ropes during the first round. Yet the champion regained his poise and remained confident. He had discovered that it was necessary to discard his usual confrontation. Instead, he adopted tactics of circling and crouching, which presented his only hope of triumphing over the towering and formidable Firpo. One may now ask, was his opponent hampered by some degree of tunnel vision? The champion, it appeared, allowed him wide berth, carefully staying within the blurred fringes of his sight.

The lesson taught by David is a simple one: no man should be daunted by seemingly immeasurable odds or encumbered by man-made rules. Greatness is hardly ever the product of conformity, overprotectiveness and security. Life's best armaments are courage and the will to achieve. When we consider thoughtfully the way in which a youthful shepherd boy slew a giant before whom an army trembled, we cannot ignore the lesson. By persevering, man can find a way ultimately to overcome any handicap; more important than size are those barriers formed by heredity and environment, especially position. David's triumph over Goliath provides a basis for understanding the meaning, which seems a paradox, of the epigram: "the race is not to the swift, nor the battle to the strong. . . ; but time and chance happeneth to them all" (Ecclesiastes 9:11).

6

Great of Will Small of Stature

And, behold, there was a man named Zaccheus, which was the chief among the publicans, and he was rich.

And he sought to see Jesus who he was; and could not for the press, because he was little of stature.

And he ran before, and climbed up into a sycomore tree to see him: for he was to pass that way.　　　　Luke 19:2-4

> *Are small men more materialistic, pragmatic, successful than large men? If so, is theirs a mechanism to compensate for what they feel is adversity?*

DO MEN SMALL OF STATURE drive to a station of success far earlier and possibly more frequently than others? Is their achievement the result of an inner drive that is physiologic; that is, tempered by *androgenic* activity? Or is it psychologic: that is, a compensatory mechanism?

In a few sentences, Luke the Physician gives us the image of a successful man of small stature and admits us into his character. Bent on seeing Jesus, Zaccheus overcame his handicap of size with characteristic determination and resourcefulness.

And when Jesus came to the place, he looked up, and saw him, and said unto him, Zaccheus, make haste, and come down: for today I must abide at thy house.　　　　Luke 19:5

Jesus had come to Jericho on His ministry—only now to become the guest of a sinner, the principal tax collector, the man most despised in the city.

Zaccheus displayed unusual agility and strength in climb-

Great of Will Small of Stature

ing the sycomore tree. He was in the right place, at the right time, and even with the right words: "Behold, Lord, the half of my goods I give to the poor; and if I have taken any thing from any man by false accusation, I restore him fourfold." To which Jesus replied: "This day is salvation come to this house" (Luke 19:8-9). Zaccheus had won the honors: he was a natural winner, even to the measure that Jesus permitted him to keep half of his worldly possessions.

Legend clothes the accomplishments of men of small stature. Court jesters were often dwarfs; their entree permitted them to influence and advise rulers. Many became privy counselors. Attila, King of the Huns and "the Scourge of God"—short, with large head, snub nose, broad chest, and deep-set eyes—was quite likely an *achondroplastic* dwarf; aggressive and ruthless, he overran Europe and knocked at the gates of Rome. Toulouse-Lautrec, the French painter, suffered from *osteogenesis imperfecta;* during his youth, his brittle bones were fractured so often that he grew up deformed, small, and twisted—a pathetic caricature of a man. Yet he would not be denied fame and success.

Strutting Mussolini and vainglorious Hitler were men of diminutive height who positioned themselves at the council tables on levels higher than those about them. Their fatuous concern about size is reminiscent of Philip the Third of Spain. Philip harbored such a deep inferiority complex that he insisted that all who addressed him do so on their knees —for the King was very short, and practically everybody with whom he had contact, courtier or peasant, towered over him. It is of some interest to observe that in today's Spain, Franco, the Chief of State, is less than five feet tall.

Napoleon Bonaparte is, of course, the classic example of the undersized aggressive man. Forcing circumstances to favor him, "le petit caporal" rose fast: a general at twenty-four and the Emperor at thirty-five, he sought to conquer all of Europe, often in the name of freedom. For a time Beethoven was taken in by Napoleon, and placed his name as Pro Consul on the title page of his Third Symphony, the great *Eroica*. But when Napoleon declared himself Emperor, Beethoven struck it off in grand anger.

Whether a success or a failure, saint or tyrant, every person is the product of his environment—a frequent theme of poets. Lord Byron's Childe Harold, for example, says: "I live not in myself, but I become / Portion of that around me. . . ." And when the aged Ulysses, leaving to his son Telemachus his sceptre and his isle, begins his last voyage— "To sail beyond the sunset, and the baths / Of all the western stars, until I die"—Tennyson has him say:

> I am a part of all that I have met;
> Yet all experience is an arch wherethro'
> Gleams that untravell'd world, whose margin fades
> Forever and forever when I move.

But every person is also the product of his heredity, as well as of his nutrition and of endemic disease; these play important roles in the molding of men, of nations, and of civilizations. Surely he is the product of the activity of his endocrine glands, for in every person they affect every cell: they influence mental acuity, physical agility, build and stature, growth of body hair and pitch of voice, sexual urges and total behavior. His endocrine system tempers man's every moment.

Not all men small of stature are resourceful and successful, of course. Nor are individuals short because of genetic and nutritional reasons alone; many are so because of a precocious output of testicular hormones—the androgens. These hasten the closure of the growing ends of bones, the epiphyses, and thus prevent further growth in stature. Small men are usually strong, agile, and aggressive—qualities that manifest good androgenic function. Maturing earlier than their fellows, yet seeing themselves as handicapped, they grasp for attainments; the taste of petty victories whets their appetites for more, nothing succeeding like success. Their triumphs spur further accomplishments and begin a process that continues throughout their lives.

Excessive tallness—when the result of good nutrition, good health, and good hereditary traits—may have its discomfitures and inconveniences, but withal many advantages, too. Tall men, when favored with a personality to harmonize with their stature, frequently become leaders of men. On the other hand, many tall men are tall because of delayed testicular activity; their full measure of growth occurs before the complete impact of testicular androgens is felt. In fact, tallness that is excessive is not infrequently a feature of the eunuchoid, who has congenitally poor androgenic or testicular function. As a result, such a man is meek and suppliant, shy and retiring, wanting force and fight.

The story of Saul, the first king of all the Jews, contrasts with that of Zaccheus. Where Zaccheus was "little of stature," Saul stood head and shoulders taller than the rest, and he was handsome: "there was not among the children of Israel a goodlier person." Yet when he was to be presented to the gathered throngs, he hid. Eventually found, he managed to stand before the people and to hear their shout: "God save the King!"—a salute which has echoed down the ages. Although King Saul was not eunuchoid, his meekness, shyness, and inordinate humility were not manly qualities, surely, and one may conjecture about the measure of his androgenic function and of his virility. At any rate, Saul proved a weak king and a failure, subject to intense and disabling psychic conflicts that at last destroyed him.

Men of diminished stature often have a compelling desire to compensate for their slightness of build by excelling in their tasks. Their drive to succeed is the by-product of heritable traits, environmental influences such as state of health and, not the least, endocrinal function.

Whereas love and charity, pity, compassion and kindly consideration are said to derive from the influences exerted by the female sex hormones common to both men and women, qualities of ambition, drive, valor, aggressiveness, militant truculence and bravado, cocksureness and acquisitiveness are said to derive from the male sex hormones. During puberty, excessive endogenous androgens will induce early sexual maturation, vigor and strength, and early closure of the growing bone ends, the epiphyses. Many short persons have the strength and the will to overcome their imagined handicap of stature.

Zaccheus, the impudent tax collector, was in the employ of the hated Roman conquerors to "render unto Caesar the things that are Caesar's." In his endeavor for wealth and power, he placed self-interest above the respect of his own people; rich and ambitious, he was known as a selfish opportunist. Yet Luke considered this man's attributes worth recording in his Gospel.

7

Righteous Indignation

And she caught him by his garment, saying, Lie with me: and he left his garment in her hand, and fled, and got him out.
Genesis 39:12

> Joseph fled from the bedchamber of Potiphar his master's wife for what reason? Was it his virtue alone? Or something else?

JOSEPH WAS A GOODLY MAN and "well-favored" when he served his Egyptian master, Potiphar, as overseer of his house, of his fields, and of all his possessions. In the routines of his business, he was exposed daily to the wiles of his master's wife, a particularly aggressive temptress. Day after day she sought to entice him, but "he hearkened not unto her, to lie by her, or to be with her." And when one day she caught him by his garment, he fled, probably in panic, leaving his garment in her hand.

Was Joseph motivated by his code of ethical behavior or, one may speculate, by fear of his sexual inadequacy? His history we may appreciate fully only if we view it from several perspectives. It is a story of morality and of triumph over adversity, but even more, a story filled with significance for the endocrinologist. Almost certainly, Joseph suffered from delayed *pubescence* together with the pangs and torments associated with retarded physical and sexual development. Deep were his emotional turmoil, his insecurity, his envy of the virility of his brothers, and the psychosexual trauma that ensued.

An impotent man disregards temptations of the flesh

more easily than a potent man. As a beautiful woman maintains her virtue with greater difficulty than an unsightly one, so a virile man must show greater restraint than one less virile. A philosopher held that "only he is virtuous who, having known both good and evil, chooses the good." By this standard, Joseph was not a virtuous man: he had not known evil as applied to carnal knowledge. He was an innocent young man in his twenties, completely lacking in experience of the way of a man with a maid.

Faced with the seductive charms of Potiphar's wife, was he unequal to the task? A young man with a clinical history of retarded sexual development naturally fears the advances of a beguiling female. Joseph could not and would not submit to the lust-thirsty wife of Potiphar, and he fled from her chamber. "Hell hath no fury like a woman scorned:" Joseph was soon adjudged a would-be rapist, and for the judgment spent three years in jail.

What evidence can we adduce that Joseph suffered from delayed pubescence and sexual inadequacy? Many of his traits indicate immaturity. Although seventeen years old, Joseph tattled on his brothers by bringing "their evil report" to Jacob, his father. He was gentle, effeminate, and handsome in a girlish way. Jacob, a man of deep insight, sought to compensate for his son's frailties by openly lavishing love and attention on him—this child of his life's twilight. Befittingly, the father made for him a "coat of many colors." The situation was one to arouse tension, and Joseph exacerbated it further by telling his dreams with special arrogance—and revelation.

A Freudian interpretation of the first of his dreams suggests clearly that he was a sexually retarded boy:

Hear, I pray you, this dream which I have dreamed:
  For, behold, we were binding sheaves in the field, and, lo, my sheaf arose, and also stood upright; and, behold, your sheaves stood round about, and made obeisance to my sheaf.
Genesis 37:6-7

Righteous Indignation

In his fantasy, Joseph found fulfillment of his wish, his craving for the attainment of manhood and of sexual potency. His longing for sexual prowess was father to the thought symbolically expressed in his dream.

His words so provoked the older brothers that they determined to be rid of him. Only the remorse of the eldest, Reuben, who still referred to the seventeen-year-old Joseph as "the child," prevented them, in Dothan, from murdering him. Instead, they sold him for twenty pieces of silver to a group of traveling Ishmaelites, who brought him to Egypt, and sold him to Potiphar, captain of Pharaoh's guard.

Prison life provided Joseph with valuable time for study, contemplation and self-inventory; there he hardened and matured. Because of his ability to interpret dreams, he was called before the Pharaoh to explain the ruler's dreams of the seven lean and the seven fat kine. Joseph predicted that seven years of plenty would be followed by seven years of famine. Pharaoh was so impressed that he rewarded him by making him the overlord of Egypt, a position of great responsibility for one but thirty years of age. Joseph grew in power and in stature. True to his prediction, plenty was followed by famine, for which he had prepared the nation. In the meantime, he wed the daughter of one of the High Priests, and she bore him two sons.

During the long famine, which also scourged Canaan, Joseph's brothers came to Egypt to buy corn. He recognized them but they did not know him, for he was now fully a man, an attainment that they could not have foreseen. Remembering his dreams of them, he twice taunted them with a meaningful reminder of his earlier handicap: "Ye are spies; to see the nakedness of the land ye are come." The repetition of "nakedness," synonym and symbol for genital exposure, is significant. Finally, Joseph revealed his identity, tearfully kissed his brothers, and brought about a reconciliation of his entire family.

Sexual immaturity, often equated with delayed pubescence rather than with a true disorder of the endocrine glands, is accompanied by mental and emotional anguish. For some, the psychic scars are erased, given time, as maturation comes. For others, their trauma, indelibly inscribed on their personalities, is forever reflected in their behavior. Secondary sex characteristics fail to develop in those with *pituitary gland* or *testicular* deficiencies. Unless substitutional hormone therapy is prescribed, the unmistakable evidence of their disorder persists throughout their lives.

Today, much may be done to promote sexual maturation. Androgens, the so-called male sex hormones, can stimulate earlier development of secondary sex characteristics, and thus circumvent the possibility of irreversible personality defects. There are those, however, who feel that nature must be allowed to take its course—and its toll. The story of Joseph provides much food for our thought; it is, in part, a clinical drama of delayed pubescence.

8

And They Sang Like Cherubs

For there are some eunuchs, which were so born from their mother's womb: and there are some eunuchs, which were made eunuchs of men: and there be eunuchs, which have made themselves eunuchs for the kingdom of heaven's sake. He that is able to receive it, let him receive it.   Matthew 19:12

> *Why emasculation? What is the role of the endocrine glands in the development of character and personality?*

FROM REMOTE ANTIQUITY, eunuchs were employed among the Orientals to take charge of their women, and among the Greeks to serve as their chamberlains. The trade of castrating boys to be sold as eunuchs for Moslem harems continued into modern times. Thus, physical changes wrought by emasculation in both man and beast have been known from the earliest period in our civilization.

What is more remarkable, however, is that 2,000 years ago Jesus recognized that "some eunuchs . . . were so born from their mother's womb." Long before the science of endocrinology became a discipline in medicine, we have recorded for us a diagnosis of congenital *eunuchoidism* or primary testicular failure.

The hormones produced by the male and female gonads have been called sex hormones because they are responsible for the development of secondary sex characteristics. However, their effects on the human organism are many, in addition to their influence on maleness or femaleness. They regulate certain aspects of metabolism, such as conservation of proteins and modification of calcium utilization, as well as affect the molding of character and personality. Eunuchs castrated in boyhood are known for their fidelity; those castrated later in life have been often suspect, correctly.

Although centuries may have elapsed before primitive people realized the relationship between sexual intercourse and the miracle of reproduction, sketches of sexual organs drawn on the walls of caves inhabited by prehistoric man attest that from the earliest times man has been fascinated by sex. The excavated walls of Pompeii and the statues adorning the temples of ancient India reveal ornamental drawings of the sex act. A bas-relief of Assyrian origin, dating back many centuries before the Christian Era, depicts a vizier and a eunuch, in which the contrast between a normal and a mutilated male is vividly portrayed. All this and the frequent references in the Bible to matters sexual testify to an appreciation of the role of sex in the daily life of man.

Replacement therapy that substitutes purified hormones for glandular deficiencies occupies an important place in the therapeutic armamentarium of today's endocrinologist. Yet the science of organotherapy had early beginnings: primitive man had notions similar to those of the modern endocrinologist, although he employed them in a vastly different fashion. He attributed great virtue to the internal organs obtained from slain enemies or from animals; the ancient warrior sought to increase his courage by eating the heart of his adversary, or to heighten his sexual power by partaking of his enemy's testicles.

For several hundred years, it was common practice to treat diseases of certain organs with like tissues from healthy animals. In point of fact, the first successful endocrine preparation was whole thyroid gland—served fried—for the treatment of thyroid deficiency. It is not surprising, therefore, that as late as 1889 the famous Charles-Edouard Brown-Sequard (1817-1894), son of an American father and a French mother and successor of Claude Bernard as

And They Sang Like Cherubs

professor of experimental medicine at the Collège de France, treated himself for waning vigor with injections of pasteurized water extracts prepared from dogs' testicles. At the age of seventy-two, this hoary-headed scientist reported his own spectacular rejuvenation before the Société de Biologie de Paris. He captured the imagination of the medical world, and his new form of therapy caught on with contagious enthusiasm.

Neither Brown-Sequard nor his students realized, however, that the testes and ovaries were unlike the thyroid in that they do not store hormones in any quantity but, instead, rapidly secrete them into the blood stream. To furnish the average dose of *testosterone*, the male sex hormone employed as a therapeutic measure, would require about one-quarter ton of bull's testes. Testosterone is synthesized in the laboratory in a pure form identical to that produced by the testes. The "good results" experienced by Brown-Sequard and thousands of other gullible males were due entirely to auto-suggestion. Worthless desiccated orchid substance (tablets of dried testicular powder) were marketed for many years before endocrinology came of age some three or four decades ago, having received a great impetus from the work of Brown-Sequard.

Although endocrine therapy was conceived in error, owing to subjective interpretation, it still opened the way for future generations to improve and perfect. Today the eunuchoid male need not be the object of such curiosity as the beardless and goat-voiced Pardoner was in the Prologue of Chaucer's *Canterbury Tales*:

> Swiche glaringe eyen hadde he as an hare,
> A vernicle hadde he sowed on his cappe.
> His walet lay biforn him in his lappe,
> Bret-ful of pardoun come from Rome al hoot.
> A voys he hadde as smal as hath a goot.
> Ne berd hadde he, ne never sholde have,
> As smothe it was as it were late y-shave;
> I trowe he were a gelding or a mare.

Today the Pardoner's condition may be remedied. The high-pitched voice, the scanty or absent beard, the poor muscular development, the lack of sexual drive, and the smallness of the *phallus*—these endocrinology may stimulate toward normalcy by vigorous treatment with pure synthetic testosterone or its analogues.

Matthew reports that Jesus spoke of "eunuchs which were made eunuchs of men." Actually, castration was practiced on man for centuries before the Christian Era, but it was practiced particularly on common farm animals in order to tame them and make them more useful for work. What was not understood was that this form of mutilation, for the best results, must be performed before maturity in both man and beast.

Castration performed on a boy results in the complete failure of development of his secondary sex characteristics; this developed the type of eunuch who was employed as the highly specialized watchman, as the guardian of the couch or the harem guard. However, if castration is performed after maturity, regressive changes of various degree, as well as a marked psychosexual upheaval, take place. Despite the castration, some individuals retain the remembrance of the sex act and do not completely lose their sexual ardor. Such eunuchs have been found *in flagrante delicti*, and when so caught were strung from the battlements. The author of Ecclesiasticus knew them, for he used the simile "like a eunuch's craving to ravish a girl" (20:4). And Aristotle (384-322 B.C.), born several centuries before the apostle Matthew, knew well that "if a full-grown bull be mutilated, he can still to all appearances unite sexually with the cow."

Castration was also practiced, on farm animals and fowl, for gastronomic reasons. Caponization of the cockerel or the rooster led to fatter and more delectable fowl for eating. The changes in the personality of the rooster are striking. The normal rooster crows, struts like the king of the walk, fights other roosters for domination, chases hens, and appears to show off his comb and wattles. Following caponization, he is docile, his comb and wattles shrink, his crowing stops, he loses his aggressiveness, and he not only plays with the hens but even, poor male that he is, sets on their eggs.

Such observations probably led to the first scientific experiments in endocrinology. Berthold of Göttingen (1803-1861), the father of experimental endocrinology, demonstrated in 1849 that the virilizing effect of the testes was actually due to endocrine activity. He found that if the removed testes were reimplanted in a different part of their bodies, the castrated cocks retained their normal appearance, sexual vigor, aggressiveness and fighting instincts, comb and wattles. He thus proved that the testis, even though severed from its nerve supply and ducts, could still, by secreting its internal secretions into the blood stream, influence both the organism and the personality.

The civilized world long ago abandoned the castration of human beings in order to make dependable and faithful servants. Yet in 1941 Dr. Charles Huggins reinstituted castration as an ameliorating measure in the management of advanced cancer of the prostate. Professor of Urology at the School of Medicine of the University of Chicago, he reasoned correctly that the prostate was hormone-dependent, and therefore that many prostatic cancers could be slowed in their inexorable progress by removal of the hormone support provided by the testes. In spite of the benefits to be derived from this procedure, some men hold dearer than life itself the possession of their testicles.

A form of punitive castration was revived in the concentration camps of Europe by the Nazi masters of sadism, to the everlasting shame of the Germanic peoples. Many an unfortunate inmate of Belzen and Auschwitz received x-ray irradiation of the testes during their protective imprisonment. Two such men, now living in the United States, were seen in consultation because of severe symptoms of the male climacteric resulting from hormone deprivation. Their testes had been removed at spaced intervals of time in order to study the tissue changes induced by x-rays. In this manner was the shameless brutality of the Nazis disguised by the mask of pseudoscience.

Finally, Jesus spoke of "eunuchs which have made themselves eunuchs for the kingdom of heaven's sake." Castration did become a religious rite. For several centuries, the choir boys of the Sistine Chapel in Rome were castrated in order to preserve their soprano voices; on reaching adulthood, such singers became known as "castrati." Only in 1878, upon the accession of Pope Leo XIII, was the Italian practice of castrating boys in order to train them as adult soprano singers brought to an end. Such famous voices as those of Caffarelli, Veilluti, and Farinelli owed their success to the abominable operation which now, fortunately, has been wholly abandoned.

In early Christian times, acting on the texts of Matthew, others voluntarily emasculated themselves, or permitted the operation to be performed on them, in order to avoid sexual temptation or sin. By the third century, a sect of eunuchs arose, the Valesii, whom Augustine describes as believing that their castration aided them to serve God. Their interpretation and practice were vehemently denounced and never officially approved by the Church. Nevertheless, religious sects have cropped up from time to time for whom castration was a rite. In 1771 such a sect, known as the Skoptsi, was discovered to exist in Russia. Their leader, Selvinov, mutilated himself as an act of salvation; he died in 1832 in his hundredth year. In 1874, it is said, the Skoptsi had more than 5,000 members. Persecuted by the Russians, they fled to Rumania. Whether this order still exists, I do not know; but this much appears certain, that the phrase spoken figuratively by Jesus of Nazareth and recorded by Matthew was taken to heart by religious fanatics in various climes and times. Jesus merely called upon those who could do so to forsake the pleasures of the flesh and to follow Him.

And They Sang Like Cherubs

The word *eunuch* appears twenty-six times in the King James version of the Holy Bible. Because of the confidence they gained from their relationship to men of importance, to kings and to princes, eunuchs frequently attained considerable stature themselves. And the word eunuch, especially in Egypt, was even applied to non-castrated, but loyal, servants and administrators of the king.

Although castration was a custom in the Orient, in the Middle East, and later in Greece and in the Roman Empire, it was not practiced by the Hebrews, according to the famous historian Josephus, on either men or animals. In all probability, Jesus would not condone so inhumane a practice as castration, for He must have known well the injunction in Deuteronomy (23:1), that the castrate "shall not enter into the congregation of the Lord."

9

Testament, Testimonial, and Testicle

And Abraham said unto his eldest servant of his house, that ruled over all that he had, Put, I pray thee, thy hand under my thigh:
And I will make thee swear by the Lord, the God of Heaven, and the God of the earth, that thou shalt not take a wife unto my son of the daughters of the Canaanites.
Genesis 24:2, 3

> *What relationship exists between taking an oath and the genitals? Why did young men of old swear on their manhood? Whence came the custom of swearing an oath on some sacred or revered object—like the Bible?*

I SWEAR BY APOLLO the physician, and Aesculapius and Hygeia and Panacea and all the gods and godesses"—thus the fledgling physician enters into a pact with mythological Greek gods that he will abide by the ethical code prescribed by the great Hippocrates for the practitioners of the healing art of medicine. To enter into convenants with the gods dates back many millenia. When the Egyptians first began to record on stone and papyrus their codes and laws, their exploits and accomplishments, their fables and foibles, such agreements were so important that they were made with gods—and thereby, of course, with people.

According to the funerary papyri, Princess Nesi-Khensu, ten centuries before Christ, contracted with the god, Amen-Ra, to grant her certain favors in the Other World in return for her zeal and devotion. A thousand

Testament, Testimonial, and Testicle

years earlier, Abraham entered into a covenant with the Lord and sealed it through circumcision. Circumcision represented a holy bond between the Lord God and this man. It is of little surprise, therefore, that Abraham in demanding an oath of his servant, bid him place his hand "under his thigh," just as today we place our hand over the heart in swearing allegiance to the flag. "Under the thigh" was, of course, a euphemism.

Why the reverence for the genital zone? Early religion, one must recall, was based on the generative impulse. The power of reproduction was of foremost importance and gave direction and consequence to religious fancies. Fecundity, of man and beasts, and fertility, of the soil, were the mainsprings of his existence, and primitive man consecrated and sanctified the organ of reproduction. He interpreted the natural phenomena about him and wove them into the imaginative social fabrics of his civilization. Day and night, the waxing and waning of the moon, the recurrent seasons, planting and harvesting, birth, death, rebirth—these fascinated him and gave meaning to his little universe. The fertility cult was grounded in the basic hopes, aspirations and prayers of his survival.

Abraham was strongly influenced by the cults, which were an integral part of the way of life of the people about him and to whose culture he had been exposed. The very mode of administering the oath that he employed was not an isolated incident, for later in Genesis we learn:

> And the time drew nigh that Israel (Jacob) must die: and he called his son Joseph, and said unto him, If now I have found grace in thy sight, put, I pray thee, thy hand under my thigh, and deal kindly and truly with me: bury me not, I pray thee, in Egypt.   Genesis 47:29

The walls of Egyptian temples of antiquity bear witness to the importance of the phallic symbol in the mores of that period. Gods, kings and great men were depicted often with penis erectus. Later, this image was translated into the obelisk, one of their popular forms of monumental design. The obelisks were much admired by the Roman emperors, and many were carried off; today they may be viewed in Rome, Constantinople, London and New York. One of the most famous, built by Rameses II at Luxor in Egypt, *circa* 1250 B.C., was transported to Paris in 1831, and five years later was erected in the Place de la Concorde. But the biggest obelisk of them all was built as a testimonial to "the father of his country," our own George Washington. The Washington Monument measures over 555 feet in height and over 55 feet at the base. It is indeed a fitting memorial to a great man who was every inch a man.

Embedded in the cultures of various peoples in widely dispersed areas of the world is a relationship between an oath and the genitals. For centuries in the Western World, man took an oath by testifying "on his manhood," and indeed the Latin word "testes" is defined in *Webster's International Dictionary* as being a witness to manhood. To testify is derived from the Latin root testis. S. R. Driver, in the *Westminster Commentary*, suggests that the Australian aborigines swore amity and willingness to aid one another by one man's sitting on the other's thighs. It is recorded that when the chief of the Sioux Indians demanded a count of the loyal warriors in his tribe, those who dropped their loin cloths did so in affirmation of their fealty.

It would appear that the custom of making a contract, taking an oath, or entering into a convenant (the literal meaning of "testament") by reference to the groin (scrotum or testes) is an ancient and common one, at any rate not confined only to the early Jews. It is found in a great number of primitive societies. This primitive form of oath-taking was long ago abandoned by the Jews and was replaced by swearing on a sacred object, such as the scrolls of the Torah (the five books of Moses). Throughout the Anglo-Saxon world, taking an oath on the Holy Bible has

Testament, Testimonial, and Testicle

become a thoroughly ingrained practice in courts of law.

In searching the scriptures, one learns that *covenant* appears many times in both the Old and the New Testaments (King James version), but that *testament*, used interchangeably with *covenant* in the New, does not appear at all in the Old. The first mention of *covenant* is in connection with Noah:

> But with thee will I establish my covenant; and thou shalt come into the ark, thou, and thy sons, and thy wife, and thy son's wives with thee.   Genesis 6:18

Testament first appears in the Gospel According to Saint Matthew, "For this is my blood of the new testament, which is shed for many for the remission of sins" (Matthew 26:28). *Testimony*, on the other hand, appears in both books, "And he gave unto Moses, when he had made an end of communing with him upon Mount Sinai, two tables of testimony, tables of stone, written with the finger of God," (Exodus 31:18).

The modern endocrinologist has an abiding interest in reproductive physiology and the effect of the hormones of reproduction on the life of individuals and their impact on the race. The course of history may have been far different if Hitler could have fathered children. There is a substantial suspicion that Hitler was asexual—his relationships to the very few women in his life were said to be platonic only. His lack of testicular vigor indirectly played havoc with his personality, and as a consequence horridly affected our civilization. It has been said of Goering, Hitler's chief lieutenant, that he behaved like an adult eunuch; he was fat and capon-like, a change that came soon after World War I. Later, frustrated, dejected, vengeful, addicted to dope and to food, he could no longer sublimate his compulsion to ravage the human race. On the other hand, vigorous men like George Washington and Winston Churchill have been mankind's benefactors. Perhaps, now that Churchill is dead, an obelisk will be built as a testimonial to him, a great and vital man—thus convenanting the hopes and aspirations of embattled and oppressed peoples the world over.

The importance of intact testicles was alluded to in Chapter 8, where mention was made that a eunuch could not enter the sanctuary. "He that is wounded in the stones . . . shall not enter into the congregation of the Lord" (Deuteronomy 23:1). This Jewish tradition was followed by the Roman Catholic Church: the sacraments of marriage and ordination were forbidden to eunuchs, and proof of intact testes became a requisite for election to the papacy.

To follow the proscription laid down in the Old Testament, legend has it that on the day of enthroning a new pope, the cardinals charged with the election of a successor to St. Peter had to verify, *de vistu et tacto*, that the "elect" indeed had testicles. According to Richard Millant in *Les Eunuques à Travers les Ages*, this task was performed while the pope, being transported on the shoulders of the canons, was seated on a marble throne with a hole in the seat. The council of cardinals then pronounced the verdict, "Testiculos habet et bene pendentes."

There is a story, apocryphal perhaps, of a young man from the mountains of Eastern Tennessee, who still spoke an Elizabethan form of English. He applied for work in a nearby city and, when asked to present his testimonials, did so by giving evidence of his manhood. Testament, testimonial and testes, indeed, have been woven into the social fabric of our civilization.

10

Token of the Covenant

This is my covenant, which ye shall keep, between me and you and thy seed after thee; Every man child among you shall be circumcised.

And ye shall circumcise the flesh of your foreskin; and it shall be a token of the covenant betwixt me and you.

And he that is eight days old shall be circumcised among you, every man child in your generations, . . .

And the uncircumcised man child whose flesh of his foreskin is not circumcised, that soul shall be cut off from his people; he hath broken my covenant.   Genesis 17: 10-12, 14

Is circumcision a religious observation alone, or is it also a matter of health?

THE ORIGIN OF CIRCUMCISION is lost in time. Yet many theories have been presented concerning it: it is a blood-offering to the gods, a substitute for other sacrifice, a hygienic practice.

CIRCUMCISION

Early in the history of the Eastern civilizations, a custom in the times of crises was to offer a human sacrifice as an appeasement to the gods or to the avenging demons. The people believed that pestilence, fire, famine, flood and earthquake were evidence of deistic wrath. Human sacrifices had been generously tempered by the substitution of animals, and it was presumed that the blood of circumcision would be an acceptable form of mollification. The expiation of guilt wrought by the blood of an individual has remained a ritualistic practice among many peoples.

In torrid lands and hot climates, *balanitis, phimosis,* and various other forms of inflammation involving the *prepuce* were common; and as protection against them, a form of surgical interference evolved. Cutting off the useless appendage with a sharp stone guarded against later irritation and inflammation, consequences of habitual uncleanliness. Circumcision mitigated the occurrence of unnecessary ills and complications, and was an aid to personal cleanliness. Tribal experience found it healthful, and it was transliterated into a form of religious purification.

Among the ancient Egyptians, circumcision was at first performed on the priestly class, then adopted by the warriors and the nobility. When Joseph became overlord of Egypt, he extended the benefits of this procedure, some scholars believe, to include the general populace. To attain this goal, he promised the Egyptians food during the famine if they would submit to circumcision. If he did so, he was the first bureaucrat to tie social security to measures for public health.

The Jews held circumcision to be of profound religious significance, for it represented the fulfillment of the Covenant between God and Abraham. With them, it became a deep-rooted custom that they could not be forced to relinquish, even during the conquest of Judea by the Greeks, and later by the Romans. It was ineradicable: when Antiochus tried to prevent the practice, mothers allowed themselves to be put to death rather than to give up the circumcision of their sons. Some rich, young, Hellenized Jews were embarrassed to frequent the public baths and gymnasia because of the stigma of circumcision; but others used it as a badge of courage.

Though John the Baptist and Jesus were circumcised according to the Law, a serious disagreement divided the early Christians. The Christians of Judea could not conceive of being converted to the new faith without submitting to the Law.

Token of the Covenant

> And certain men which came down from Judea taught the brethren, and said, Except ye be circumcised after the manner of Moses, ye cannot be saved.   Acts 15:1

All of Apostle Paul's tenacity and persuasiveness were necessary to prevent circumcision from being made a condition to membership in the New Order. It was decided not to put a yoke upon the neck of the disciples, not to insist on circumcision—an alien concept, difficult for the Gentiles to accept. Thus the Apostles settled for the following minimum, but necessary things, so as to lay upon them no greater burden: "That ye abstain from meats offered to idols, and from blood, and from things strangled, and from fornication: from which if ye keep yourselves, ye shall do well" (Acts 15:29). As Christianity spread through the Occident, circumcision was all but lost to the Christian world. Yet in the last few decades, pediatricians and obstetricians have revived its practice throughout the western world.

CIRCUMVENTION

Many years ago, visiting St. Peter's Hospital for Stone, in London, I was spectator of a difficult surgical operation for genital malignancy. The gray-haired surgeon remarked that, in his long experience, he had never encountered penile cancer in a Jew. I pondered this observation, searched through the literature, and found the case report of a Jew who did suffer from this form of cancer; however, born and bred in a small town in Nebraska, he did not have the rite available to him and was never circumcised. On further inquiry, I learned that in India, genital cancer is much more frequent in the Hindu than in the Mohammedan; the latter is circumcised as a ritual of puberty.

Circumcision is a worthwhile procedure, it would appear, if for no other reason than its prophylactic value. But there is greater import to this observation than is immediately apparent, and that concerns the epidemiology of cancer of the mouth of the womb, that is, the cervix. Nuns and virginal women rarely have cervical cancer, thus incriminating a factor of married life, coitus.

According to a ten-city survey, the incidence of cancer of the cervix in American white women is 35.2 per 100,000, in American non-white women, 61.2 per 100,000. In Israeli women, the rate is 2.2 per 100,000, and this exceedingly low rate is matched by studies on Jewish women in the United States. The significance of these facts has not been appreciated fully. Among women in most Latin and South American countries and among Hindu women in India, cancer of the cervix accounts for about 40% of all malignancies in the female. The most likely common denominator is the introduction through coitus by the uncircumcised sexual partner of a cancer irritant or virus.

There is almost certainly more to circumcision than mere ritual. The historic experience of the peoples inhabiting the Fertile Crescent and the lands bordering the shores of the eastern Mediterranean has provided a clue that may contribute much to unravelling the *pathogenesis* and *epidemiology* of both penile and cervical cancer.

CIRCUMSPECTION

There may have been other motives for circumcision. The foreskin protects the sensitive *corona* and *glans*. Exaggerated sensibility of these structures may initiate a train of reactions, in the unconscionable and undisciplined individual, detrimental to the mores of society. Circumcision permits greater *cornification* and thus diminishes the *hyperesthesia* of the glans. By dulling the edge of sensuousness, man is better able to bridle his passions and to adjust his sexual behavior to conform with convention.

The priapic preoccupation of the early Israelites with the foreskin was inspired as much by the goal of survival as by reasons spiritual and aesthetic. Through trial and error, the forerunners of our Judeo-Christian civilization learned of the expediency of circumcision; it became a religious rite, but it was a good public health measure.

11

At the Point to Die

And Jacob sod [boiled] pottage: and Esau came from the field, and he was faint:
And Esau said to Jacob, Feed me, I pray thee, with that same red pottage; for I am faint: . . .
And Jacob said, Sell me this day thy birthright.
And Esau said, Behold, I am at the point to die: and what profit shall this birthright do to me?
. . . and he sold his birthright unto Jacob.
Genesis 25:29-33

> *Did Esau sell his birthright cheaply, as the Scriptures suggest, despising it? Or did he have a physiologic need greater than that for his birthright?*

MORE OFTEN MISREAD than any other Bible story, perhaps, is that of Esau, heir to his family birthright because he was born before his twin brother, Jacob. This elder son of Isaac and Rebekah is maligned as an insensitive glutton who unhesitatingly traded his most precious possession for a mere bowl of pottage. Yet none suggests that he wanted either intelligence or ambition: surely such a man would have appreciated the honors and possessions that his birthright assured to him.

Esau's words of assent to Jacob's hard bargain are dramatic for the modern endocrinologist, and for his patients. "Behold," he said, "*I am at the point to die:* and what profit shall this birthright do to me?" In almost certainty, Esau was the victim of an illness recognized only in recent times: *hypoglycemia*, or low blood sugar.

The discovery of the hormone *insulin* in 1921 by the late

Sir Frederick Grant Banting, Nobel laureate, opened a great medical era. It made possible, finally, the successful management of those persons afflicted with uncontrollably high blood sugar, *diabetes mellitus*.

But after physicians had employed insulin for several years, an astute clinician, Dr. Seale Harris of Alabama, observed in some of his patients signs and symptoms like those that result from an overdosage of insulin. And with Dr. Harris' observation, a new clinical entity came into being: the syndrome of low blood sugar, known as hypoglycemia.

Its symptoms vary, but most evident are hunger and a craving for sweets, sometimes accompanied by fatigue and weakness, apprehension and confusion, blackouts and even stupor. A decline in blood sugar triggers an outpouring of *adrenalin*, which so stimulates the body's sugar stores that they are released into the blood stream. Such is our built-in adjusting mechanism that keeps our essential blood sugar at fairly constant levels.

However, as adrenalin enters the blood, it may cause palpitations of the heart, flushing and sweating, or syncope (a fainting spell). Victims feel, surely, "at the point to die." Such a victim was Esau, who seemed to know his limitations and his needs: he knew that he must have food and water instantly, or drop. He really had little choice between trading his birthright for the mess of pottage and getting well, or going without the pottage and suffering the ignominy, for a cunning hunter, of total collapse. Observe how readily he recovered:

> Then Jacob gave Esau bread and pottage of lentiles; and he did eat and drink, and rose up, and went his way: thus Esau despised his birthright.   Genesis 25:34

Did Esau despise his birthright? Formerly, the diet given to one threatened by an impending attack of low blood sugar was food rich in *carbohydrates* and starches. But many years of experimenting with diets proved that the longtime management of the disorder was dependent not on high carbohydrates but on high-*protein* feedings. The protein-rich lentil soup that Esau craved provided a clue long unnoticed and so unheeded.

Sugar-starvation is a strange illness, and until Dr. Harris defined it in 1924, it belonged in the category described by Camillo in *The Winter's Tale* (I, 2):

> There is a sickness
> Which puts some of us in distemper; but
> I cannot name the disease. . . .

Even today its diagnosis is often missed because of the extreme variability of its manifestations. The occurrence of functional hypoglycemia, although frequent enough, is understood so poorly that the disorder has earned the soubriquet, "stepchild of medicine."

It is marked by an increased output of, or increased sensitivity to, endogenously produced insulin. This sensitivity is intensified by emotional turmoil and stress, by constant pressure and by violent exercise. We know today that the syndrome of low blood sugar stems from various endocrine disorders—pituitary gland failure, severe *hypothyroidism* (myxedema), exhaustion of the adrenal glands (Addison's disease)—but that the most severe cases are caused by the somewhat rare insulin-producing tumors of the pancreas.

Recently, hypoglycemia has been recognized as a complication in some cases of *congenital adrenal hyperplasia*, a disease that Esau might well have had. In this disease, because of an inborn error of metabolism, the adrenal gland produces an excess of hormones that virilize the female and cause the male to undergo a precocious development of secondary sexual characteristics (macrogenitosomia praecox). These hormones are produced at the expense of essential cortisone-like hormones that are necessary to the body's economy in maintaining salt and water balances, and that profoundly influence the storage and utilization of sugars and of fats. Congenital adrenal hyperplasia exists in at least four types: the normal group (no apparent salt and water imbalance), the high blood-pressure group (salt-retainers, hypertensives), the salt losers (tendency to shock and acute crises), and the low blood-sugar group (hypoglycemia).

Esau's history suggests that he was a victim of hypoglycemia, probably as a complication of congenital adrenal hyperplasia, with its associated macrogenitosomia praecox. Such a child is often robust, an "infant Hercules." His early growth is rapid: his muscular development, his strength, and the size of his genitals are abnormal, his voice is extremely deep, and he is very hairy. Yet, paradoxically, in spite of all these signs of extraordinary virility, he is, like Esau, subject to sudden collapse.

The twin brothers had struggled within Rebekah's womb as they were to struggle without:

> And the first came out red, all over like an hairy garment: and they called his name Esau.
> And after that came his brother out, . . . and his name was called Jacob: . . .
> And the boys grew: and Esau was a cunning hunter, a man of the field; and Jacob was a plain man, dwelling in tents.
> Genesis 25:25-27

They were of startling contrast: one rough, the other polished; one a strong hunter, the other a homebody. Small wonder that "Isaac loved Esau . . . but Rebekah loved Jacob." So deep was her mother's love for her favorite son that she stooped to deceit and, that he might win the blessing of his aged and blind father, persuaded Jacob to disguise himself as his brother by dressing in goat skins.

> And Isaac said unto Jacob, Come near, I pray thee that I might feel thee, my son, whether thou be my very son Esau or not.
> And Jacob went near unto Isaac his father; and he felt him, and said, The voice is Jacob's voice, but the hands are the hands of Esau.

At the Point to Die

And he discerned him not, because his hands were hairy, as his brother Esau's hands: so he blessed him.   Genesis 27:21-23

Having himself foresworn his birthright, Esau now lost all opportunity of recovering it.

Although low blood sugar is labeled a "modern disease," it is rooted clearly in antiquity. The body's priceless commodity, sugar fuels the cells and sustains the brain; without it, the body fails. Esau may offer us the first recorded case of hypoglycemia, and we may be impressed by his knowledge of its quick corrective—the high-protein lentil soup and bread of barley and of wheat.   He was a husky huntsman, the scripture indicates, who loved life, lived it to the hilt, and had little choice but to sell his birthright when "at the point to die."

12

A Little Bit of Salt

And it came to pass, that, as I made my journey, and was come nigh unto Damascus about noon, suddenly there shone from heaven a great light round about me.
And I fell unto the ground....   Acts 22:6, 7

> *Did Saul of Tarsus, later Paul the Apostle, suffer from heat prostration because of depletion of salt and water, or from something else?*

THE COURSE OF HISTORY has often been altered by some unforseen event, some psychophysical happenstance or ailment occurring in an individual destined to influence the lives of his own and future generations. It is said that Napoleon might have won the Battle of Waterloo had he not been so discommoded, the previous night, by the pain and discomfort of a severe case of hemorrhoids that he was late for the battle. If the Berbers in Africa had not revolted against the Arabs soon after Charles Martel stopped the invading Mohammedan hordes at Poitiers in 732 (Battle of Tours), Martel might not have contained the surging Moslems and thus saved Europe for Christendom. If Saul of Tarsus, tormentor of those Jews who had accepted Jesus of Nazareth as their Messiah, had not fainted on his journey to Damascus, he might not have undergone conversion to the New Order and become Christianity's great protagonist.

Let us examine the circumstances of Saul of Tarsus' frightening experience under the relentless noonday sun, while on his long and arduous journey to Damascus from Jerusalem.

A Little Bit of Salt

Brooding over the manner in which he persecuted his fellow Jews, Saul was impressed by their "turn thy other cheek" attitude to his abuse. He probably drank little and ate little while on this journey. In all probability, he was the victim of heat prostration owing to depletion of salt and water. What was uppermost in his subconscious came to the fore as he heard a voice saying: "Saul, Saul, why persecutest thou me?" (Acts 22:7) Because of the aura —the forewarning that comes before an epileptic seizure, in this case the "great light"—students of the life of St. Paul have ascribed this disorder to him. Did Saul of Tarsus suffer an epileptic attack? Recovery from an attack is usually a matter of minutes. But in Saul's case, the severe and damaging effect of heat prostration lasted three days. He was in a stupor and so grievously affected that during this time "he was three days without sight, and neither did eat nor drink" (Acts 9:9). Later, relating his experience to Agrippa, Paul once more emphasized that the spell occurred at midday while the sun was very bright.

> At midday, O king, I saw in the way a light from heaven, above the brightness of the sun, shining round about me and them which journeyed with me.   Acts 26:13

So eloquent and convincing was Paul concerning his mission and his fealty to his heavenly vision that Agrippa is reported to have said: "Almost thou persuadest me to be a Christian" (Acts 26:28).

In all hot climates, the syndrome of heat exhaustion from salt and water depletion is common. Heat exhaustion presents a typical picture of salt depletion—muscular weakness, headache, giddiness, tendency to faint on standing, loss of appetite, nausea, vomiting, cramps, mental confusion and delusions. The treatment is salt replacement, and today salt tablets are provided for those exposed to strenuous work or exercise in the heat. Incidentally, long before adrenal cortical hormones became available, Dr. Jacques Loeb managed his patients with Addison's disease by advising a marked increase in salt intake. Dr. H. L. Marriott of London, England, in his book *Salt and Water Depletion*, relates that during a tour of duty in India, 1,959 men were hospitalized because of heat prostration, and 136 died.

The body's electrolyte balance can be seriously injured in hot atmospheric conditions by loss of water and salt from sweating, overheating from cessation of sweating accompanied by a very high fever (hyperpyrexia), or water depletion without salt loss. If neither water nor food is taken, the effects of water depletion dominate the picture; unavoidable water losses continue while salt loss is relatively slight. The body economizes salt more effectively than water. Pure water depletion occurs in the shipwrecked and those lost in the desert.

The importance of salt and water balance in the body economy may be judged from the fact that the imbalance may readily terminate in death. Salt and water are so closely associated in the body that their constancy must be maintained at precise levels by a most intricate system of checks and double checks. The posterior pituitary gland's antidiuretic hormone conserves water; the adrenal cortical hormones, aldosterone and other corticoids, conserve sodium (salt); and the kidneys preserve the chemical balance in the body by monitoring the reabsorption or elimination of necessary elements.

We live in an "internal sea" of fluids. Our entire internal environment passes through the kidneys 15 times a day. Approximately 1,700 quarts of blood flow through the kidneys every day, but only one-thousandth is converted to urine. Far less dramatic than the throbbing of the restless heart are the Herculean labors of the kidneys. Their task is prodigious but silent, regulating the vital salt and water balances within extremely narrow limits compatible with life. About two and one-half pounds of salt pass through the kidney tubules daily, but only a little less than one-third of an ounce is excreted in the urine. Thus our internal sea, the body fluids, serves as an ever-present reminder of our marine ancestory.

Before their first stirring in the primeval slime, the extremely remote ancestors of man lived in the briny deep. To come ashore, they had to establish an enclosed aqueous medium that would carry on the role of sea water. That man's forebears evolved from the sea may be assumed from man's developing a most complex and remarkable system in order to maintain the internal environment—in a fashion to match, more or less, the salinity of his ancient abode.

Snively points out, in his excellent *Sea Within: The Story of our Body Fluid*, that our chemical ancestry can be traced ultimately to the earth, for the chemical properties that made it possible for life to arise in the sea were washed there from the solid earth. Jesus of Nazareth meant more than it seemed when he said, in the Sermon on the Mount: "Ye are the salt of the earth" (Matthew 5:13).

We can rejoice with the Psalmist who with solemn reverence sang: "How manifold are thy works, O Lord," when we learn of the crucial role that the body fluids play in the physiologic drama of our daily lives. The very body fluid, described as converted sea water, is delicately brought into balance despite the extreme changes in atmospheric conditions and food intake.

Salt's essential usefulness to man caused it to be referred to often in the Bible, literally and figuratively. Salt has played a decided role in the history of mankind. It was greatly valued in the preservation of fish and meat and as a dietary supplement. In lands where cereal foods are the main source of nutrition and the diet is poor in salt, the addition of salt is necessary to maintain vigorous health. The importance of supplementary salt became part of the religious custom of the ancient Jews, and to this day the salting of the first morsel of bread as part of the grace before a meal is followed by Orthodox Jews throughout the world. The preservative qualities of salt made it a peculiarly fitting symbol of an enduring race ("a covenant of salt . . ." Numbers 18:19).

Salt held great economic importance. It was the main source of trade between many nations. In Oriental countries, salt taxes were so heavy that the article was not infrequently mixed with inert materials and reached the consumer in an impure state. The reference in Matthew 5:13—"if the salt have lost his savour"—takes on meaning. In the Roman army, an allowance of salt was given to the officers and men. This "salarium" had the equivalence of money. The expression "not worth his salt" may be equated with "not worth his salary". One of the oldest roads in Italy is the Via Salaria, by which the produce of the salt pans of Ostia was carried into the Sabine country.

The word *salt* is sprinkled throughout the entire Bible. It is found in both the Old and New testaments, appearing over 35 times. A land sowed with salt became uninhabited and useless (Deuteronomy 29:22, 23). A land abundant in salt reserves was chosen by Moses for the children of Israel as the Promised Land.

And as for the western border, ye shall even have the great sea for a border: this shall be your west border (Numbers 34:6).
And the border shall go down to Jordan, and the goings out of it shall be at the salt sea: this shall be your land with the coasts thereof round about (34:12).

The role of salt in the health and survival of his people was of consummate importance to Moses. Moses led the children of Israel to the land of promise; he understood well the arid country, the intense heat, the heavy labors and struggles ahead. As an Egyptian prince, he observed the fatigue, heat exhaustion and death that came to the Israelitish slaves who toiled in the broiling sun, preparing "bricks without straw" (Exodus 5:7) for their Egyptian masters. Fully aware of the necessity of salt to the health

A Little Bit of Salt

of his people, he made salting part of the rites and rituals for the preparation of food, especially meat. The availability of salt tablets to men working in great heat is now saving countless lives.

It appears that a little bit of salt or the lack of it may have changed the course of history. Saul, after collapsing in the noonday sun, was compelled by the voice he heard and the vision he saw to convert to the new order.

It must be recalled that by the time Saul of Tarsus took on his evangelistic mission, James, the brother of Jesus, was already established as the leader of a small but active community in Jerusalem. Though the early followers believed in Jesus as the Messiah (Christos), they were observant Jews according to the "law of Moses" (Acts 21:20). Neither James nor Peter was wholly in accord with the aggressive policies advocated by Saul, soon to be known as Paul. His goal was to bring the message to a larger arena of people—the gentiles. With indefatigable zeal he set out to accomplish his purpose amid unbelievable hardships and considerable hostility, by presenting the new *ethic* in a more palatable and acceptable form.

We will never know what might have been the course of history if James had had his way. Peter reluctantly accepted the Pauline doctrine. This much is certain, that the dramatic change in Saul's cerebration was indirectly responsible for the seeding and growth of Christianity throughout the Mediterranean World.

13

Signs and Symbols

> For nothing is secret, that shall not be made manifest; neither any thing hid, that shall not be known and come abroad.
>
> Luke 8:17

Whence come symbols? Are they the secrets of the past speaking to us? Do we know their meanings?

SIGNS AND SYMBOLS leave their stamp on posterity. An idea portrayed by a mark, letter, work, emblem, insignia, or other token may serve as a symbol. If attached to it are some attributes and it sparks the imagination and arouses the emotions, anything may be symbolic. Symbolism may involve the art of selecting, consciously or unconsciously, analogies for the abstract. Most familiar to us are flags and coats of arms, school and college crests, and symbols connected with certain ideologies and religions. Although symbols are a great part of our world, we seldom realize their impact on our thoughts and our actions.

Symbols are the common language of people, literate and illiterate, the world over. They are a language that incites and excites, implies and implores, informs and stirs, often plumbing deep wells of emotion. Their original meanings often lie lost beneath the dusts of centuries. For example, at one time a red shield marked both the home and place of business of a petty banker—Mayer Amschel of Frankfurt-on-Main. In translation, the house with the red shield is now the "House of Rothschild." In Germanic countries, a green leaf ("grune blatt") was the hallmark

Signs and Symbols

of a hostelry or inn, where it was possible to learn the events taking place in both neighboring communities and the outside world. Thus, it follows logically that a widely read German weekly—a scandal or gossip sheet carried on in the tradition of a news-gathering hostelry of old—is known as the *Grune Blatt*. The sign of the three golden balls, which today is displayed outside the pawnbroker's shop, was the proud "neon sign" of the first bankers of the modern world, the Medici family of Florence.

What does Rx on a prescription mean to the average physician, medical student, or pharmacist? Whence the insignia of the general's star, the colonel's eagle, or the major's cluster of oak leaves? How did the caduceus—the rod entwined by one or two snakes—become the emblem of the healing arts?

Among the best-known symbols today is the physician's emblem—"Rx"—which has been employed since ancient times. It is believed that this was originally the symbol of *Marduk*, god of wisdom, who became Babylon's chief divinity. His sign was placed on prescriptions by Babylonian physicians, who used it as an invocation to him. Such a practice can be traced back to more than ten centuries before the Christian Era. It is probable that a general's star was adopted, perhaps unconsciously, from an ancient belief that stars held a special power. In fact, stars were worshipped by the people of certain nations, including Egypt and Chaldea. The Chaldeans, interested in astrology, revered the stars, and their brilliance so impressed the Israelites that they made them symbols of exalted persons, like King David, the Patriarchs, princes, rulers, and nobles. Besides denoting nobility, they served as guides, as in the story that a star in the East guided the Wise Men to the place of Jesus' birth. Since a general is a distinguished person and a guider of men, this symbol is fitting. A full colonel's emblem, *the silver eagle*, had ever denoted greatness and power; the rapidity of an army's movements is compared with an eagle's flight in the Old

Testament. Gaius Marius, a Roman general who lived during the century before the birth of Jesus, chose an eagle as the sign to be used on the banner of his legion. Under the French Empire, it became France's emblem also. The oak leaves, worn by both a lieutenant colonel and a major, can be traced far back. The tree is Israel's symbol signifying strong, powerful men. Or perhaps it was chosen because of its later connection with the famous British Oak in Sherwood Forest, called the *Major Oak* during the time of King John, son of Henry II.

Greek medicine set the stage for later centuries. The ancient Greek physicians were the priests of Aesculapius, who practiced in temples. Although Aesculapius was deified, he had been an actual man dedicated to healing, and his symbol was the *caduceus:* two snakes twined around a rod (this famed physician's name is also spelled Asklepios). He lived during the 13th Century B.C., and is honored by being included in the oath of Hippocrates taken by medical students. The physician's insignia, the caduceus, might have originated from the belief held by ancient Greeks that serpents were divine and associated with the art of healing. Therefore, snakes were housed in the temples of Asklepios. That great physician is depicted as holding a rod, around which a snake is curled. Greek mythology contains numerous stories of serpents with healing powers. The rod was supposedly given to Mercury, herald of the gods; poets have written that it brought sleep. In *Paradise Lost,* John Milton termed it "his opiate rod." During the 18th century, Erasmus Darwin wrote of Hermes (the Greek predecessor of the Roman Mercury) as using his "dread caduceus" as a means of rescue "From the dark regions of the imprisoned dead...." Possibly the roots from which the symbol of the caduceus originally sprang mingled magic with religion. Today, it bears a different significance: the snakes indicate "wisdom in healing," and the rod or staff is a token of "comfort and compassion." This emblem was employed by

Signs and Symbols

the Royal Army Medical Corps and later became the emblem of this country's Army Medical Corps. Thus antiquity reaches toward our day through the common language of symbolism.

Subconsciously, words, paintings, designs, and architectural structures are part of the language of symbolism. The cross in early civilizations signified solar light. The vestments of the priests of Horus, the Egyptian god of light, were marked with a cross. It was the monogram, too, of Osiris, the chief Egyptian god, and implied Nature's productive force. With the crucifixion of Jesus, the cross became the symbol of Christianity. The swastika, a design revered in ancient India, was once a token of health and happiness, but the cross twisted into the shape of a swastika, adopted by Nazi Germany, will be remembered for a thousand years as a symbol of hate, of the abrogation of human rights, and of contempt for the dignity of man.

One's consciousness seems to be a ceaseless flow of symbols, and unconscious energies continuously seek expression. From man's earliest times on earth, he has sought in one way or another to portray his idea of God and of sex. Is the lofty church spire transmuted phallic worship? Is the dome of the mosque the subconscious expression of a woman's nuturing breasts? Is the inverted triangle, the emblem of the YMCA, an imitation or replica of the female escutcheon? After all, the early Jewish Christians veered from a rugged and militant philosophy to a credo that emphasized such maternal attributes as love, kindness, compassion, faith, hope, charity, "turn the other cheek" and peace above all things.

These gentle virtues were urged on the Gentiles, who frequently were unprepared to receive them. Some 19 centuries later, the female escutcheon—pure and inviolate, representing femininity and gentility—was unconsciously translated into a symbol of communal welfare and endeavor. And what of the significance of the star of

David, emblematic of many Jewish organizations today? Was the six-pointed star subconsciously allied with the male escutcheon in its equation with virility and fertility? Perhaps the male escutcheon superimposed on the female remains an historic reminder of the fertility cults that flourished in ancient times and was the font of man's earliest religious experiences.

Indeed, symbols speak to us from out of the past with nuances that words cannot intone.

> And thou shall bind them for a sign upon thine hand, and they shall be as frontlets between thine eyes.
> And thou shalt write them upon the posts of thy house, and on thy gates.   Deuteronomy 6:8, 9

This exhortation in Deuteronomy was taken literally. An amulet containing passages from the scriptures is to this day worn on the forehead and arm of many Orthodox Jews during their morning prayers. It is a symbol of a covenant with the Lord to keep his commandments for a better life and a better world.

We are in continuous need of reminders—how else can we explain the phenomenon of the "Beatles" other than as a symptom of our times. We live, we say in a sick, sick, sick world; but is it sicker than other times? Has there ever been an era when the forces of good were not challenged by the forces of evil? Conflict—national and international—follows closely upon conflict; one hate group emerges as another agonizingly dies, and world crises on end bring us to the brinks of many wars. Hate often seems stronger than love, and justice unceasingly tries to catch up with injustice. Yet man's compassion for his fellow man can surpass man's inhumanity to man. And the need for such a reminder by a fitting symbol on our gateposts has not lessened with the ages.

Many Jewish homes throughout the world have a "Mezuzah"—a small metal casing enclosing a passage of Scripture—as a sign on the door post. It serves as a wel-

Signs and Symbols

come to "the stranger within our gates." This gesture has been perpetuated also, by some Christian orders. A small wooden symbol, a "House Blessing Cross," may be found at the rear entrance door of St. Joseph's Hospital in Augusta, Georgia—an institution administered by the Sisters of St. Joseph (Carondelet):

>   LORD
>   AND
>   MASTER
>   PROTECT THIS HOUSE
>   AND EVERYONE WHO GOES
>   IN
>   AND
>   OUT

14

Seven and Seven

> And at that time, Solomon held a feast, and all Israel with him, a great congregation . . . before the Lord our God, *seven* days and *seven* days, even *fourteen* days.   1 Kings 8:65

> *What meaning do* seven *and* fourteen, *which recur throughout the Bible, shadow forth?*

FOURTEEN AND SEVEN appear often in the Old and the New Testaments, especially in the apocalyptic writings. Veiled in mystery, their uses often defy interpretation, yet both carried special meaning, clearly, in the remote past. Can it be that manifested in them as symbol is some centuries-old inheritance, from the bedrock of human experience? May the symbol be an unconscious reminder of some gratifying discovery, now all but forgotten, a haunting remnant of a joyous association of time and event? And may the endocrine system offer a key to unlock some part of our answer?

The Bible has a rich supply of these numbers; they fall into three categories: mystic, pragmatic, physiologic. Several of the New Testament uses are inscrutable. In giving the genealogy of Jesus, for example, Matthew's fourteen is considered by scholars to be symbol rather than measure of time:

> So all the generations from Abraham to David are fourteen generations; and from David until the carrying away into Babylon are fourteen generations; and from the carrying away into Babylon unto Christ are fourteen generations.   Matthew 1:17

Seven and Seven

We must also read as symbol Paul's years: "I knew a man in Christ above fourteen years ago," 2 Corinthians 12:2.

Symbolic must remain the sevens of The Revelation of St. John the Divine, which is centered on seven. Its scenes are in a sevenfold structure: seven vials, plagues, trumpets, thunders, heads which are mountains; seven kings, crowns, and a slain lamb with seven horns and seven eyes. One of its clearest verses is (1:20):

> The mystery of the seven stars which thou sawest in my right hand, and the seven golden candlesticks. The seven stars are the angels of the seven churches: and the seven candlesticks which thou sawest are the seven churches.

Yet the numbers often are employed clearly and definitely. In his Epistle to the Galatians, Paul wrote: "Then fourteen years after I went up again to Jerusalem" (2:1); again in the Acts when, shipwrecked and hungry, he appeals to the passengers to partake of food: "This day is the fourteenth day that ye have tarried and continued fasting, having taken nothing" (27:33). And in the Old Testament fourteen appears with explicit meaning: the ledge of the altar shall be "fourteen cubits long and fourteen broad" (Ezekiel 43:17); Jacob served Laban fourteen years, seven for Leah, seven for Rachel (Genesis 31:41)—these from many examples.

The *Holy Days* of Judaism, which originated in Biblical times and are still celebrated, are built on sevens. The seven days of *Passover* begin at sundown on the fourteenth day of the prescribed month. The second great annual festival, the *Feast of Weeks*, begins seven weeks after Passover. And the third, the *Feast of Tabernacles*, is held in the seventh month. Most important of all is the *Sabbath*, Judaism's great contribution to human welfare, a day for rest, contemplation, and worship: "And God blessed the seventh day, and sanctified it" (Genesis 2:3).

What physiologic meanings may seven and fourteen possess? Moses, the great lawgiver, may well have understood the significance of the fourteenth day of the menstrual cycle as having something to do with fertility. He so desired the Children of Israel to multiply that he may well have contrived to increase the fertility index of Israelitish women by his ordinances of the Law of the "Clean" and the "Unclean," as in Leviticus 15:

> This is the law . . . of her that is sick of her flowers (32-33)
> And if a woman have an issue of her blood . . . she shall be unclean (25).
> But if she be cleansed of her issue, then she shall number to herself seven days, and after that she shall be clean (28).

Women were asked to offer a sacrifice on the eighth day and encouraged to bathe in running water and be purified. Thus, after five or six days of menstruation and a waiting period of eight days, the woman was cleansed and prepared for her marital obligations, just when the likelihood of conception was greatest, on the fourteenth day of the cycle. Whether this practice was born of knowledge, prophetic vision, or of tribal experience, Moses apparently was aware of the importance of the fourteenth day of the cycle in reproduction and in the preservation of the race.

When the scribe used "seven days and seven days, even fourteen days" to describe Solomon's feast, his usage was probably less poetic modality than emphasis of an obscure symbol. Seven occurs more often than three, fourteen, or forty, the numbers heaviest with symbolism; and it seems to carry more meaning. For seven is intimately associated with the natural rhythms of nature. At four multiples of seven, the moon waxes and wanes. The periodicity of the menstrual cycle follows the lunar month. There is rhythm in the rounds of the sun, the stars, and the moon, and a periodicity to many a biological phenomenon, particularly in the endocrine system. The rhythm of all human life, according to Dr. Hobart A. Reimann, may be controlled by the solar cycle of 6.6 days.

All these relations are pertinent to the folklore and sig-

Seven and Seven

nificance of the number seven. Seven possesses magic: *seven days of creation, seven ages of man, seven deadly sins, seven joys of Mary, seventh son of seventh son, seven wonders of the world, seven seas, seventh heaven, seventh year: sabbatical, seven hills of Rome*—and seven and seven are fourteen.

Past is prologue, an introduction with a theme that is partly clear, partly blurred, partly forgotten. Its symbols, though they may seem worthless to a scientific era, speak, still. All that ever was still is. And we would do well, pausing, to turn from the demands of our days to listen and learn from that which is as old as time yet everlastingly new. So with seven and fourteen: mystical numbers, symbols, through which antiquity whispers of a buried treasury of wisdom awaiting our discernment.

15

A Little Wine

Drink no longer water, but use a little wine for thy stomach's sake and thine often infirmities.   1 Timothy 5:23

> Has man's use of wine and of spirits been for his weal or for his woe?

WINE'S ANCIENT WORTH and its curse are mentioned almost two hundred times in the Bible. Although the Apostle Paul's advice to Timothy was to use wine for a medicinal purpose, its intoxicating character was known. The "Dry Bible" substituted the word *juice* for *wine* in order to obviate the scriptures' slightest encouragement to drinkers of wine.

The important role of wine in the Jewish mores and social customs is illustrated by Jesus' first miracle. When the supply of wine ran out at the marriage feast in Cana of Galilee, Jesus, at the behest of his mother, turned water into not wine, but "good wine," so that the festivities could proceed (John 2:1-10). So doing, He was abiding by a Jewish custom that holds wine to symbolize the joy and fellowship of a happy occasion, and that, even now, is a part of the Jewish marriage ceremony.

Because the origin of winemaking is lost in the past, we do not know when man discovered that the juice of the grape, if allowed to ferment, becomes wine. But we know that neolithic man, turning from hunting to agriculture, used his crops for fermentation, and that people in various parts of the earth learned that grapes or wet grain, allowed to stand in warmth, became a liquor that possessed weird and pleasant effects. Rock carvings and sketches from as early as the fourth millenium B.C. depict the technics used in winemaking. The world's first biochemists, probably, were those not-so-primitive people who concerned themselves with the fermentation of grain for beer, or of grapes for wine.

To some early men, the blood of the grape had supernatural powers and contained, or was, a "spirit." Wine and religion were soon entwined, and wine became a part of various ritual ceremonies. At the Last Supper, when Jesus and his disciples were celebrating the Feast of the Passover, Matthew relates (26:27-28):

> And he took the cup, and gave thanks, and gave it to them, saying, Drink ye all of it;
> For this is my blood of the new testament, which is shed for many for the remission of sins.

Thus began the practice of communion or the Eucharist in Christian churches.

The ancient Hebrews mixed wine and water for their beverage—"she hath mingled her wine"—and the Greeks and their cultural heirs in Rome embraced this gentle custom. In olden times, pollution of streams and of wells caused frequent epidemics of cholera and of dysentery; slowly, experience passed from one generation to another that to drink water plain was hazardous. The addition of wine to water was a safety measure; to ingest mingled wine was healthful.

The reasons for the initial popularity of wines among the peoples that border the eastern and the northern shores of the Mediterranean have become dim, but the custom continues. With Gallic delight, the French have always maintained that wine is for drinking and water is for washing. A cartoon depicting a child's posterior being washed carries the legend, "La seule utilité de l'eau." Pasteur rightly described wine as the most hygienic of beverages.

The prophylactic measure of adding wine to water was

thought to be a sort of myth, a popular practice handed down from antiquity. But in his charming and scientific book, *A History of Wine As Therapy*, Dr. Salvatore P. Lucia shows that it is a good deal more. Dr. Alois Pick, of the Vienna Institute of Hygiene, exposed to various mixtures of wine and water the bacilli that caused cholera and typhoid fever—two diseases transmitted by drinking water—and discovered that in them the bacilli were soon destroyed. Further, in World War II, enteric diseases spread by contaminated water presented a severe medical problem in the Mediterranean theater. An American soldier, John Gardner, was impressed by the fact that the natives, who added wine to their water, were free from enteric diseases. Later, in a series of studies at the University of California, he found that red wines possess antibacterial properties that cannot be ascribed to their content of alcohol, aldehydes, tannins, and acids. Finally, investigations by John J. Powers at the University of Georgia, in 1959, proved that other elements extracted from wines also inhibit the growth of bacteria.

That wine has antibacterial power independent of its alcohol is now well-established, and the wisdom of the ancient custom of mixing wine with water is substantiated by scientific inquiry.

Wines were drunk with meals, during festivities, and for ritual purposes, generally in moderation. But scandalous excesses did occur. The earliest reference to wine in the Bible points out that such excesses lead to confusion and abnormal behavior:

And Noah began to be a husbandman, and he planted a vineyard:
And he drank of the wine, and was drunken; and he was uncovered within his tent. Genesis 9:20-21

Noah's sons were so embarrassed that they "covered their father's nakedness."

For health's sake and to avoid inebriation, the Hebrews

A Little Wine

had learned to dilute their wine with two parts of water; unwatered wine they considered too strong, and they permitted no blessing until the water was added. Proverbs, a poetic discourse in which man stands torn between wisdom and folly, has this to say about mingled wine:

> Wisdom hath builded her house, . . .
> . . . she hath mingled her wine; she hath also furnished her table.
> . . . as for him that wanteth understanding, she saith to him,
> Come, eat of my bread, and drink of the wine which I have mingled.
> Forsake the foolish, and live; and go in the way of understanding.
> Proverbs 9:1-2, 4-6

Wisdom dictates moderation if man would forsake the foolish. To be alive is not always to live, as physicians realize in the course of any day. Living requires concerns far more vital than biological processes only, and any excess thwarts the adventure, challenge, and love that make man more than an animal. And the best can be twisted into evil; wrong usage and intemperance always haunt man.

That wine may be a tool for vice Lot's daughters illustrate. Following the destruction of Sodom and Gomorrah, Lot and his two daughters lived in an isolated cave in the mountains. Fearful of the future, the daughters schemed:

> And the firstborn said unto the younger, Our father is old, and there is not a man in the earth to come in unto us after the manner of all the earth:
> Come, let us make our father drink wine, and we will lie with him, that we may preserve seed of our father.
> And they made their father drink wine that night: and the firstborn went in, and lay with her father; and he perceived not when she lay down, nor when she arose.

So, also, with the younger daughter, and thus "were both the daughters of Lot with child by their father" (Genesis 19:31-36).

The prophets took a dim view of drinking wine. One

of the sternest, Hosea, spoke at a time when Israel neglected God, and his indictment is stinging:

> ... the Lord hath a controversy with the inhabitants of the land, because there is no truth, nor mercy, nor knowledge of God in the land.
> Whoredom and wine and new wine take away the heart.
> Hosea 4:1, 11

The Bible denounces the immoderate use of wine. Advocating moderation in all things, Paul wrote:

> All things indeed are pure; but it is evil for that man who eateth with offence.
> It is good neither to eat flesh, nor to drink wine, nor anything whereby thy brother stumbleth, or is offended, or is made weak.
> Romans 14:20-21

Paul here indicates that wine is evil only if man makes it so, and that those who drink normally are not to tempt the weak. His was probably the first preventive measure suggested to curb problem drinking; his appeal is to the strong "to bear the infirmities of the weak, and not to please ourselves" (Romans 15:1).

If Paul attempted to cope with problem drinkers, Isaiah defined the source of the problem as a guide to those on the brink of or far gone in alcoholism:

> Woe unto them that rise up early in the morning, that they may follow strong drink; that continue until night, till wine inflame them!
> Woe unto them that are mighty to drink wine. . . .
> Isaiah 5:11, 22

We know today that the morning drinker has entered the labyrinth called alcoholism; Isaiah's picture of the night-and-day drinker is precise. But perhaps the most completely descriptive of the denunciations is that of Proverbs:

> Wine is a mocker, strong drink is raging: and whoso is deceived thereby is not wise (20:1).

A Little Wine

Be not among winebibbers; among riotous eaters of flesh:
For the drunkard and the glutton shall come to poverty: and drowsiness shall clothe a man with rags (23:20-21).
Who hath woe? who hath sorrow? who hath contentions? who hath babbling? who hath wounds without cause? who hath redness of eyes?
They that tarry long at the wine; they that go to seek mixed wine.
Look not upon the wine when it is red, when it giveth his color in the cup, when it moveth itself aright.
At the last it biteth like a serpent, and stingeth like an adder (23:29-32).

This passage is an accurate description of one who has fallen into the fearful abyss of alcoholism. It no way concerns the normal drinker, to whom alcohol is a means and not an end. Herein is the test by which one may determine whether he is a potential or even an actual alcoholic. If alcoholic beverages are but a means to one's moderate relaxation, refreshment, and stimulation, and an adjunct to hospitality, then he is hardly in danger. But if alcoholic beverages become an end, if they are a salve for one's problems, and if he drinks compulsively, then he is on treacherous land. One drink is too many—a hundred not enough.

Although general opinion has it that one becomes an alcoholic only after years of overindulgence, I believe that some persons are born with a predisposition for alcoholism, that a tendency to it is within their genetic structure. For them, warning signals flash early: they drink more than their companions, more often, more compulsively, for the wrong reasons.

Although the drinking of wine received its share of condemnation, in praise of wine the psalmist sang: "Wine maketh glad the heart of man" (Psalms 104:15). And in Proverbs 31:4-7, King Lemuel's mother makes a nice distinction for its use:

It is not for kings, O Lemuel, it is not for kings to drink wine; nor for princes strong drink:

Lest they drink, and forget the law, and pervert the judgment of any of the afflicted.

Give strong drink unto him that is ready to perish, and wine unto those that be of heavy hearts.

Let him drink, and forget his poverty, and remember his misery no more. Proverbs 31:4-7

The Talmud, written between 536 B.C. and A.D. 427, offers another sort of description, of a woman consuming too much wine:

One glass of wine makes the woman pretty; two glasses and she becomes hateful; at the third glass she lusts invitingly; at the fifth glass she becomes so excited that she will solicit an ass upon the streets.

This remarkable estimate one may compare with Emil Bogen's alcohol-behavior relationship: One-tenth per cent and the lady is delightful and desirable, two-tenths and she is daring and disheveled, four-tenths and she is delirious and disgusting, five-tenths and the lady is drunk. And one recalls the porter's conclusion in Macbeth (II, 3): "and drink, sir, is a great provoker, . . . it provokes the desire, but it takes away the performance."

Some centuries after Mohammed, a stirring in science and philosophy occurred in the Moslem world. The Arabs welded Judaeo-Christian thought to that of the Graeco-Roman civilization, and the result was an energetic inquiry into metaphysics and science. The learned sought, among more important things, to discriminate the essence of wine and to capture its hidden magic. Seeking to isolate the "spirit" of fermented juices, inquisitive Arabs of the eighth century developed a technic in which wine was heated, then cooled and condensed to prevent the vapor from escaping. The result was distilled spirits, more potent than the wine—quite unneutral "neutral" spirits.

Since the discoveries of fortifying wine and distilling liquor, the problem drinker—a problem then as now—has become more prevalent. Why is it that one person becomes drunk with one or two drinks while another maintains his poise after four or five? Why is it that alcoholism is a metabolic disorder in one and a psychiatric problem for another? Our answers are not too complete.

We do know that the hypothyroid person oxidizes alcohol more slowly and is therefore more likely to become inebriated on a few drinks. The hypoglycemic person (and the hypothyroid has a distinct tendency to hypoglycemia) may inadvertently learn that alcohol, just as food or sweets, gives him a quick boost. In individuals with emotional instability, this boost may even lead to alcoholic addiction; they become psychologically conditioned to the use of alcohol as an escape mechanism. Because of malnutrition, the chronic alcoholic develops poor liver function, which interferes with the storage and release of glycogen, which leads to low blood sugar—and the vicious cycle runs on.

A relationship has been suggested between endocrine disturbances and alcoholism. In one series of problem drinkers studied, two-thirds had some degree of hypothyroidism; after thyroid therapy, their drinking patterns became less pathologic. The effect of the thyroid hormone was recently re-examined, using this time the quick-acting thyroid substance l-triiodo-thyronine (Cytomel). The drinkers given the hormone were clinically sober within two hours, their rate of blood-alcohol decline approximating clinical sobriety; the drinkers not given the hormone took from four to six hours to become equally sober.

Wine is cheering, nourishing and stimulating, and is probably the drug and the medicine with which humanity has had its longest experience. Wine and alcohol in moderation are a tonic to the aged, a help in promoting appetite, and a comfort to living at a time of increasing physical infirmities and diminishing satisfactions. They help to relax chronic anxieties because they placate the troubled spirit and rest the racing mind. Certainly, before science devised a variety of specifics to ameliorate diverse ailments, wine was an indispensable boon to mankind. Even in Ancient Egypt, wine was employed as a vehicle for so-called remedial agents, and many a popular nostrum today owes its success to the beneficial action of the wine or the sedative effects of the alcohol.

Wine is a highly complex product. Of it, Dr. Lucia writes:

> As food, wine supplies fluids, calories, minerals, vitamins, proteins, and other dietary elements. As medicine, wine may act as an appetite stimulant, a stomachic, tonic, tranquilizer, anesthetic, astringent, antiseptic, vasodilator, diaphoretic, diuretic, and antibiotic agent, in addition to its age-old use as a universal menstruum for active therapeutic agents derived from plants.

And Dr. William Dock has concluded that physicians are not fully using wine at its clinical value:

> Alcohol is a good diuretic, a stimulant of gastric secretion, a dilator of blood vessels, and above all, it has an action on the mind which, by variation of dose and rate of ingestion, can bring either cheerful bustle or profound anesthesia.

Dr. Samuel Johnson knew wine, whisky, and brandy: "In the bottle," he wrote, "discontent seeks for comfort, cowardice for courage, and bashfulness for confidence." He considered that "there is no doubt that not to drink wine is a great deduction from life," and that "Wine makes a man better pleased with himself. . . . To make a man better pleased with himself, let me tell you, is doing a very great thing." But he gave it up, "till I grow old and want it," for the best of reasons: "because it is so much better for a man to be sure that he is never to be intoxicated, never to lose the power over himself."

Paul's "use a little wine for thy stomach's sake and thine often infirmities" embodies the best thought of his time. The observant Jew still offers a grace before partaking of

A Little Wine

a glass of wine: "Praised be thou, O Lord, King of the Universe, who hast created the fruit of the vine." Wine is indeed a gift from the gods, participating as it does in the sublimest of religious mysteries, though perversely contributing to the depths of human debauchery and degradation. Wine and alcohol are not the undoing of man; they are, when he permits them, his helpmeets, his servants. But they have the power to uncover the frailty of the human fabric whenever it is unable to weather the stresses and the storms of life.

16

Give Yourself to Fasting

In those days I Daniel was mourning three full weeks.
I ate no pleasant bread, neither came flesh nor wine in my mouth, neither did I anoint myself at all, till three whole weeks were fulfilled.   Daniel 10:2, 3

> *Why has fasting persisted through the ages? Are its effects harmful or beneficial?*

THE PRACTICE OF FASTING has persisted from time immemorial, and it is likely to continue so long as men are capable of religious and moral aspiration. Rooted in some of the strongest emotions incident to human nature, it is a form of masochism surrounded by an aura of self-denial, -purification, and -sacrifice. The first mention of fasting in the Bible concerns Moses on Mount Sinai: for him, it was a rite of purification, of preparation for spiritual communion.

And he was there with the Lord forty days and forty nights; he did neither eat bread nor drink water. And he wrote upon the tables the words of the covenant, the ten commandments.   Exodus 34:28

To endure so prolonged a fast is difficult to imagine. The fast that Jesus undertook, when "led up of the spirit into the wilderness to be tempted of the devil," also lasted forty days and forty nights. The tempter asked Jesus to command the stones to be made bread. His answer reverberated down the ages: "Man shall not live by bread alone" (Matthew 4:4). In early times, the ascetic, in his efforts to

Give Yourself to Fasting

subdue carnal desires, withdrew from all distractions of daily life and abstained, wholly or in part, from food; he hoped thereby to be free for spiritual thought and introspection. Fasting was a part of the religious ritual of many of the ancient cultures; the Old and New Testaments mention it seventy-four times. Penitential fasting is found today particularly in the Jewish and Christian faiths.

In Islam, the fast of Ramadan is a universally observed thirty-day sunup to sundown self-imposed period of food restriction, a modified fast. Buddhists find fasting appropriate to their way of contemplation and asceticism.

In different lands and ages, the practice of fasting has been differently applied. The New Testament records ". . . for there lie in wait for him of them more than forty men, which have bound themselves with an oath, that they will neither eat nor drink till they have killed him . . ." (Acts 23:21). Among the Celts, it was not uncommon for a man who was refused a lawful request to "fast against" the one who had denied him his right.

In more recent times, fasting has been used as a means of protest against alleged injustice, legal or political—namely, the hunger strike. A notable example was that of Viterbi, the Corsican lawyer condemned to death for political causes. Viterbi went on a hunger strike and provided, through a carefully kept diary, an inkling of the effects of voluntary privation. On the third day of fasting, he noted that the sensation of hunger departed, and although thereafter thirst came and went, his hunger never returned. His death occurred on the eighteenth day.

The most renowned faster of modern times was Mahatma Gandhi. In his passive resistance to the British rule of India, he engaged in fifteen fasts, three of them lasting for twenty-one days. He usually had for sustenance only hot water, sometimes with lime juice, and although he grew very weak, he remained mentally alert and suffered no lasting ill-effects. Terence MacSwiney, the Irish patriot and Lord Mayor of Cork, protested his sentence of two years' imprisonment by the British by going on a diet of water alone for sixty-nine days. He died a martyr's death in October, 1920, but not because of his fasting: he died of pulmonary tuberculosis aggravated by his long deprivation of nourishment. Fasting is for the obese relatively easy; for the lean it is far more difficult.

Observations were made on the prolonged fasts of "professional fasters" toward the end of the last century. Scientific studies of the physiology of hunger and of the metabolic and psychologic changes that occur on prolonged fasting were started both in this country and abroad early in this century. In 1915, Benedict published the results of his studies of a man who, drinking only distilled water, fasted for thirty-one days. About the same time, Cannon, professor of physiology at Harvard, was carrying on his monumental studies on the effects of fear, rage, pain and hunger on the body economy. Cannon showed the concept "hunger increases as time passes" to be erroneous:

On the contrary, there is abundant evidence that the sensation is not thus intensified. During continued fasting, hunger, at least in some persons, wholly disappears after the first few days.

Four or five decades passed before the fruits of such studies were clinically applied. Dr. Walter Bloom demonstrated that total fasting with free access to water was tolerated well and, in fact, most beneficial as an introduction to the treatment of obesity. In a recent report, Dr. Garfield Duncan and his associates corroborated Bloom's work and gave evidence of the practicable application of intermittent periods of total fasting, except for non-nutritious fluids. Such fasting was followed within a few days by *anorexia* and frequently by *euphoria*. Low caloric diets failed because they stimulated hunger rather than anorexia. Furthermore, the loss of salt and of water noted on total fasting failed to occur on low caloric diets. The impression that hunger stressed the individual, resulting in increased corticoid activity by the adrenals, thus heightening catabolism

Give Yourself to Fasting

or breakdown of tissue proteins, was not substantiated by hormone assays performed before and after total fasting periods of four to fourteen days. A relationship was found, however, between the anorexia and the degree of ketosis (a mild form of acidosis in the faster's bloodstream).

Modern medical science, examining this ancient practice of total fasting, has found that it is a safe, painless, effective method for the obese individual, if undertaken for one to several weeks while under the care of a physician. It helps him to mobilize fat, which burns or is metabolized into fatty acids—hence the ketosis. Only the preoccupation of man with eating at regular intervals has led to the misconception that fasting is unpleasant. However, it is most difficult for the lean to fast, since they have little fat reserve; it must have been a particularly difficult trial for men like Gandhi and MacSwiney. In the lean, the ketones, which lessen hunger, are not produced as they are in the obese, in whom fats are readily mobilized.

Obesity is a menace to health and happiness. Nevertheless, Shakespeare, in alluding to the fat and the lean in *Julius Caesar* (I, 2), lets Caesar epitomize an opinion held by scholar and layman alike ever since man started to record his ideas in picture and word. The consensus of myth, legend, history and drama has overwhelmingly equated obesity with good-naturedness and leanness with shrewd, self-critical, calculating ruthlessness.

> Let me have men about me that are fat;
> Sleek-headed men and such as sleep o' nights.
> Yond Cassius has a lean and hungry look;
> He thinks too much: such men are dangerous.

Voluntary fasting, an age-old practice, has become a therapeutic tool in the control of intractable obesity. Fasting for ten to fourteen days, given access to water, is neither archaic nor barbaric. It is tolerated well by obese men and women, and is a revolutionary and promising approach to the management of obesity.

17

Fallen Angel

When I consider thy heavens, the work of thy fingers, the moon and the stars, which thou hast ordained;
What is man, that thou art mindful of him? and the son of man, that thou visitest him?
For thou hast made him a little lower than the angels, and hast crowned him with glory and honour.   Psalms 8:3-5

> *What is man, what woman, and what are the physiologic errors each is heir to?*

THE IMPORTANCE of "What is man, that thou art mindful of him?" may be judged from the fact that it is one of the few passages to be found, word for word, in both the Old and the New Testaments (Hebrews 2:6-7). The two aspects of man ever have been the concern of the civilized world: man's soul and man's body. Out of the mouths of babes come queries that tax the ingenuity of scholars, such as that of the little child: "What is an angel?" I am sure that the query is directed at the physical appearance and the gender of an angel, not at his ethereal and spiritual qualities.

But when the philosopher poses the question, "What is man?", I know of no better reply than that of Homer Smith: "As a fallen angel, man would be ludicrous. As an intelligent animal he has reason to be proud, because he is the first who can ask himself, Whither, Why, and Whence?"

The poet, the historian, the social anthropologist do not inquire of physical man only, but of man endowed with a soul. God breathed life into the nostrils of man that he might rise to a position a little lower than the angels, and

Fallen Angel

seek truth, do justly, love mercy, and walk humbly with his God. These things men should be and do, as Tennyson's King Arthur instructs the last of his knights, Sir Bedivere:

> If thou shouldst never see my face again,
> Pray for my soul. More things are wrought by prayer
> Than this world dreams of. Wherefore, let thy voice
> Rise like a fountain for me night and day.
> For what are men better than sheep or goats
> That nourish a blind life within the brain,
> If, knowing God, they lift not hands of prayer
> Both for themselves and those who call them friend.
> For so the whole round earth is every way
> Bound by gold chains about the feet of God.

The evils wrought by man, his lapses from reason when he detaches himself from human goodness, are the expressions of his baser self. The beast in him comes to the fore as an atavism that blocks the brotherhood of man and of nations. But a glimmer of hope breaks through the clouds of darkness that enshroud our universe; for the nobility of man shines forth time and again by precept and example. Human compassion glowed in the hearts of uncounted men and women who risked their lives to rescue Jews from the Nazi executioners. How can we reconcile the depravity of the Nazi in espousing mass murder with the humaneness of the Dutch and of the Danes? Nowhere, in no other period of history, has the ennobling quality of compassion been more clearly demonstrated than in the decency and heroism of thousands of men and women of France, Belgium, Norway, Italy—and Germany, too—who harbored and hid many a person intended for the furnaces of Buchenwald or the gas chambers of Auschwitz. Indeed, fallen angels have distorted man's image and purpose.

Shakespeare's Hamlet suggests man's condition, his glory and his almost-nothingness (II, 2):

> ... this goodly frame, the earth, seems to me a sterile promontory, this most excellent canopy, the air, ... appears no other

thing to me than a foul and pestilent congregation of vapours. What a piece of work is man! How noble in reason! How infinite in faculty, in form and moving! How express and admirable in action! How like an angel in apprehension! How like a god! The beauty of the world! The paragon of animals! And yet, to me, what is this quintessence of dust? Man delights not me,—no, nor woman neither, though by your smiling you seem to say so.

Shakespeare was only too aware of the baser side of "this quintessence of dust"—his tragedies are replete with vengeance, murder, incest, hate and violence—and his Hamlet, again, asks the crucial question:

> What is man,
> If his chief good and market of his time
> Be but to sleep and feed? A beast, no more.

Seen not from the lofty perch of the theologian or the social scientist, but from the lowly pedestal of the endocrinologist, man has another side. The endocrinologist, too, asks "What is man?" except that he adds, "And woman, also?" For the endocrinologist is occupied with glandular and genetic influences that make man or make woman. An error in one or the other may so change physical make-up that the true identity of the individual is confused.

The factors that separate man from woman are tenuous. The endocrinologist recognizes true *hermaphrodites* with gonadal structures of both the male and female, and with external genitalia that are in a mixed state of development. He is aware of male and female pseudohermaphrodites; that is, persons with gonadal organs of one gender and incompletely differentiated external genitalia. He sees demi-females with failure of developmental growth of the ovaries, *Turner's syndrome,* and demi-males with very poor testicular development, frequently complicated by breast growth, *Klinefelter's syndrome.* And he finds males who think and act like females, and females whose aptitudes and attitudes are masculine, regardless of their sexual structures.

Fallen Angel

The normal female has twenty-two pairs of non-sex *chromosomes* or *autosomes* and an XX sex *chromosome complex*, resulting in the normal human chromosome compliment of forty six. The normal male has the same number of autosomes and an XY sex chromosome complex, for the total of forty six. In the demi-females of Turner's syndrome, one-half of the XX complex is lost, so that they possess only forty-five chromosomes. In the demi-male of Klinefelter's syndrome, an extra X is present, so that the sex chromosome complex is XXY for a total of forty-seven chromosomes.

Some individuals have all the appearances, instincts and drives of the female, yet harbor in their abdominal cavities testes instead of ovaries (the syndrome of feminizing testes). Their chromosomal pattern is similar to that of a male, but their bodies and minds belong to the female. Needless to say, these genetic anomalies may work havoc with the body form as well as with the personality, thus debasing the soul.

In a discussion of "What is man?", we must look back to our very beginnings, and ponder the written word: "So God created man in his own image, in the image of God created he him; male and female created he them" (Genesis 1:27). Metaphorically, we may assume that original man, Adam, was hermaphroditic. Such an assumption is quite permissible, for it is twenty-one verses after reporting the creation of man—how many millenia later I do not know—that Genesis (2:18) tells us:

And the Lord God said, It is not good that the man should be alone: I will make him an help meet for him.

In the history of human events is thus recorded man's earliest conception of the establishment of the sexes. Some of the most distinguished Hebrew writers, according to Selye, interpret the first chapters of Genesis as describing Adam as being of both sexes.

Hermaphroditus was a minor Greek divinity, half-man half-woman, the continuation of legend. But far from being the objects of worship and veneration, his unfortunate human successors became the objects of scorn and derision. The latter-day Greeks cast them into the sea. Legend has it that in Basle in 1474 even a cock was sentenced and burned at the stake for the heinous and unnatural crime of laying an egg. Thereabouts, too (Geneva, 1553), Michael Servetus, discoverer of pulmonary circulation, was burned at the stake.

Hermaphroditism has left an indelible imprint on the ladder of evolution, it seems, and its baneful legacy occasionally crops up in man. The different stages in the development of the individual reflect in a dimly vestigial manner some of the principal ancestral forms from which the species is descended. The earliest embryonic stages resembled the most remote ancestors. Now, the opprobrium has been extended to individuals who, save for their inability to reproduce their kind, have all the appearance and appurtenances of either maleness or femaleness.

Much may be done today to compensate for the glandular or genetic error. Removal of gonadal structures not in harmony with the instinctive drives of the individual, together with administration of replacement hormone therapy to develop the appropriate secondary sex characteristics, has met with considerable success. Also, surgery of the external genitalia is performed to enable the patient to conform with the laws of nature. Many such unfortunate individuals may be restored to semi-normalcy so that they may walk, head high and unbowed, with their spirits unbroken because of an error in development. Fate plays many tricks, and there is indeed a destiny that shapes our ends.

Some lay people and men of the cloth, as well as physicians, feel that interference, surgical or hormonal, with such individuals is against the will of God. Such arguments are not new and apply not alone to developmental abnormalities of man. When the Erie Canal was being built, there was strong opposition to it, even on religious grounds. Harry Emerson Fosdick relates that at a Quaker meeting a

Fallen Angel

solemn voice was heard: "If God had wanted a river to flow through the State of New York, He would have put one there." After a few moments of profound silence, another member rose and said simply, "And Jacob digged a well." An eloquent and sobering statement, something that reactionaries might well ponder.

Man is body and soul. Each influences the other. Man must rise above the common herd, the sheep, the beast in the field. Glandular and genetic disorders distort the image of man. When evolutionary reminders do crop up, they may, in a measure, be remedied. Notwithstanding the atavistic manifestations, man's animal instincts must forever be sublimated if our civilization is to endure. Man must indeed strive to be only "a little lower than the angels."

18

A Vessel Full of Vinegar

And the soldiers also mocked him, coming to him, and offering him vinegar.   Luke 23:36

> *Why does "vinegar"—from the dawn of civilization a benefit to man as a medicine and as a condiment in preparing and preserving his food—connote unpleasantness?*

THE VINEGAR OF BIBLICAL DAYS actually was soured wine and, though not particularly pleasant to the taste, refreshing. It was the beverage of the tiller of the soil, the field hand, the soldier on the march. In dry, arid climes it served as a prolonged thirst quencher; in World War II, vinegar was added to the canteens of soldiers who were deployed in areas where water was scarce, so that the supplies would last longer.

Wine vinegar and apple-cider vinegar are relatively rich in potassium, a substance vitally important in the body's chemistry. Could it be that the ancients unknowingly replenished potassium stores by its ingestion? The cumulative experience of tribal man led him to assume that such a drink also helped to lessen fatigue; recent researches have elucidated partially the role of potassium in energy exchange. Writing in the second century, Galen—some authorities say he was a thousand years ahead of his time—recommended for fatigue a concoction of vinegar, honey, and water.

One of the early references to vinegar in the Bible is in the story of Ruth (2:14):

A Vessel Full of Vinegar

And Boaz said unto her, At mealtime come thou hither, and eat of the bread, and dip thy morsel in the vinegar. And . . . he reached her parched corn, and she did eat, and was sufficed. . . .

The psalmist, however, regarded the vinegar drink as something considerably less than ambrosial. When weary, troubled, and in search of some comfort, he was chagrined by the offer of this refreshment. He cried out:

Reproach hath broken my heart; and I am full of heaviness: . . . and in my thirst they gave me vinegar to drink.

Psalms 69:20-21

Thus we observe the ambivalent regard in which vinegar was held—both as a delight and as a despair.

Vinegar has been employed in the healing arts throughout the centuries, for both internal and external uses. By 400 BC, it was well established as a medicament, frequently prescribed by Hippocrates. The mildly acid property of vinegar evidently proved to be a bacterial inhibitor, for it was empirically employed in the treatment of wounds and bruises. Dioscorides (AD first century) washed his hands in vinegar before undertaking a surgical procedure. The uses of vinegar have not altogether lessened with time and have become part of the folk medicine of our day.

In an age of unbelievable advancement in all branches of science, folk medicine often is discounted as superstitious nonsense. Yet many a simple remedy, which at first seems illogical and irrational, ultimately justifies its use. So with snake root, lowly weed, valued by Hindus as a soporific, and used by Gandhi to allay his anxieties during his political crises. What seemed a victory of mind over fact has been hailed as a "modern miracle" drug. Reserpine, the active alkaloid of snake root, was isolated from this weed and is the basis for one of the most important tranquilizing agents, *Serpasil*, also an effective suppressant of high blood pressure. From foxglove, a brew of which was imbibed by simple English country folk with heart disease and dropsy, has come *digitalis*, the mainstay in today's management of the failing heart.

In the Middle Ages, an aromatic vinegar of Marseilles became known as *le vinaigre de quatre voleurs*, thought to be endowed with sovereign efficacy against plague and pestilence. According to the confession of four thieves who had plundered dead bodies during the plague at Marseilles, this preparation prevented them from contracting the disease while pursuing their nefarious trade.

Once it was fashionable for English physicians to carry a gold-headed cane as a symbol of their profession. During the 18th century, the head of the cane became known as a "vinaigrette," because the doctors put a tiny bottle of aromatic vinegar within the hollow knob and, when visiting the sick, inhaled the fumes to defend against contagion. Hogarth, famous artist and satirist, left to posterity an engraving which caricatured a group of well-known quacks of the day in sober consultation. Several are shown sniffing at their canes—"to each sagacious nose applied."

The uses of vinegar are legion. It is the douche universal. Mixed with clay, it is a poultice for swollen joints. It is a gargle for sore throat and an application for skin ailments —particularly the *dermatitis* that erupts beneath *orthopedic* casts—to toughen the skin and to prevent and treat sunburn. And many a young mother knows that the pungent odor of the soiled diaper may be prevented by submerging the diaper in a pail of water to which she has added vinegar: the vinegar neutralizes the alkaline ammonia.

In recent years, Dr. D. C. Jarvis has brought renewed interest in vinegar to this country through his popular book, *Folk Medicine*. He concluded that the unusually rugged health of Vermonters is gained by their traditional mealtime drinking of a mixture of water and apple cider vinegar (with honey, if desired). He reasoned that vinegar must be beneficial to man and beast, since he has repeatedly witnessed farm animals dig into and eat the soil on which mother of vinegar had been poured or spilled from an old

A Vessel Full of Vinegar

keg. Dr. Jarvis believes, contrary to current medical opinion, that this old New England nostrum has withstood the test of time and is a preventive medicine or a remedy for countless ills. Its incorporation into the feed of horses and of cattle is said to enhance their fertility and to improve the sheen of the coat and the gloss of the hide.

In Biblical days, the analgesic benefits of wine vinegar, when mixed with myrrh, frankincense, mandrake, or other herbal drugs such as gall, were well known. In the gospels, Matthew and Mark differ about the drink proffered to Jesus; that is, whether it contained gall or myrrh. "And they gave him to drink, wine mingled with myrrh: but he received it not" (Mark 15:23). There is reason to believe that it may have been gall (*Papaver somniferum*), an opium-poppy plant which thrives in the Holy Land, from which was derived a drug that eased suffering and induced sleep. Over the years, leading theologians from diverse branches of Christianity have joined other scholars in maintaining that this soothing liquid was offered to Jesus by the Daughters of Jerusalem, a small group of Jewish women dedicated to acts of charity and mercy. Deploring the Roman introduction of crucifixion, a deadly sin according to Jewish law, they prepared the anodyne to dull and stupefy those about to die by this inhumane form of execution. After Jesus was sentenced by Pontius Pilate, He was led away—

> And there followed him a great company of people, and of women, which also bewailed and lamented him.
> But Jesus turning unto them, said, Daughters of Jerusalem, weep not for me. . . .   Luke 23:27, 28

When the analgesic drink was proffered to Jesus to lessen his anguish, He refused it; He had resolved to endure the full measure of his suffering. "They gave him vinegar to drink, mingled with gall: and when he had tasted thereof, he would not drink" (Matthew 27:34). Finally, as the agonizing hours took their measure, Jesus said, "I thirst." It was then that one of the Roman soldiers, moved to compassion by the heroic endurance of their political prisoner, soaked a sponge in vinegar and held it up to Jesus. This time there was no additive of herbal drugs.

> And straightway one of them ran, and took a sponge, and filled it with vinegar, and put it on a reed, and gave him to drink. Matthew 27:48

To quench their own thirst, the Roman soldiers kept a supply of the beverage within easy reach. Because all four gospels agree, we may assume that the vinegar was at hand and that its usefulness was known well.

Some years ago, in California, a condemned man asked and received a pint of whiskey from Governor James Rolfe, Jr. The Governor had consulted with the chaplain of the legislature—Rabbi Norman Goldburg, now of Augusta, Georgia—who assured him that to offer the condemned a drink to mitigate their suffering was traditional. Although the "righteous" flayed their Governor, one may wonder whether it is ever too late to dispense the milk of human kindness, even when the milk is alcoholic. Did not Jesus, in His final moments on the cross, taste of the wine of vinegar, to moisten His parched lips and to assuage His thirst?

Medicinal and restorative properties of soured acid wine have been known, then, since antiquity. This wine has served as an inexpensive and satisfying beverage, as a prolonged thirst-quencher, as a zesty condiment, as a vehicle by which the powers of herbal pain relievers are enhanced, and as a readily available and reportedly effective remedy for boundless ills. The progress of modern medicine has not dimmed the enthusiasm for vinegar as a household remedy for a host of illnesses of man and beast. The soured wine of the Bible has indeed enjoyed a useful, colorful and bizarre role in the history of mankind.

19

Woman's Destiny

> Now Abraham and Sarah were old and well stricken in age; and it ceased to be with Sarah after the manner of women.
>
> Genesis 18:11

Need the climacteric end a fruitful life?

ALL THE DAUGHTERS OF EVE experience three phases in their progression through womanhood: puberty, the reproductive years, and the climacteric. The *menarche* outwardly manifests that pubescence is about to end and that the reproductive years are at hand. The *menopause*, the cessation of the menses, heralds the beginning of a change in the way of life, from fertility to the end of reproductive potential. Menstruation is regarded as a normal physiologic process—an imaginative gynecologist once called it "the womb weeping for the cast-off ovum" —but it is also a destructive process, frequently accompanied by toxic reactions, and is truly Nature's curse on Eve.

The loss of fertility at the cessation of menses was recognized in antiquity. The Old Testament records that Sarah, wife of Abraham, conceived at an age so advanced that it had ceased to be with her "after the manner of women." She displayed the symptoms linked to the change of life; cantankerous and irritable, she probably upbraided Abraham often. Her life had passed her by, and she had no proof of her womanhood to leave to posterity. She accused Abraham of being sterile and, challenging him, urged him to "go in unto my maid." Now it is not at all improbable that, in her menopausal state, Sarah urged with contempt, having every reason to believe him sterile. But Abraham accepted, "went in unto Hagar, and she conceived."

Thus was devised an early practical test to prove male fertility. Distasteful as it may seem today, it has not been discarded altogether. The realization of the importance of the male component in the study of infertility eludes many physicians, and often they neglect to evaluate the *seminal* status of the male partner.

When Hagar conceived, Sarah, vexed and hurt, in envy and despair sent the bondwoman away from her domicile. It was then that the Lord mercifully opened Sarah's womb: she bore a son and his name was Isaac. This birth is mentioned several times in the New Testament; Paul records it in this manner:

> And being not weak in faith, he [Abraham] considered not his own body now dead, when he was about an hundred years old, neither yet the deadness of Sarah's womb.   Romans 4:19

The resumption of *ovulation* in middle-aged women who have not menstruated in several years is encountered occasionally. *Uterine* bleeding, on the other hand, in women well past their menopause, does occur in the presence of hormone-producing ovarian tumors, and is noted also in hypertensives and in women with blood dyscrasia.

Several years ago, a woman of fifty-seven, who had migrated from Iraq to Israel, there ate fava beans for the first time. Her urine became tinged with red, and was interpreted as menstrual flow. Now, fava beans contain a chemical component that, on ingestion, so sensitizes the red blood cells of certain Mediterranean people that they undergo dissolution. When, in the following spring, she came down with severe *hemolysis* and red-colored urine, she again blamed the Holy Land for its known miraculous effect on aged women. One may recall that Sarah, too, came from what is now Iraq as she journeyed from Ur of the Chaldees to the land of Canaan.

Sarah's attitude towards Hagar was a departure from the

graciousness that characterized most of her life. In her impatience and anguish, she also showed her worst self in reproaching her husband:

> And Sarai said unto Abram, My wrong be upon thee: I have given my maid into thy bosom; and when she saw that she had conceived, I was despised in her eyes: the Lord judge between me and thee.
>
> Genesis 16:5

Was Sarah's behavior part of the menopausal syndrome? The menopause is a rung of the ladder of a woman's progression through life, the climacteric, the change of life. During it, her balanced ovarian function declines and her menstrual flow ceases; she steps from reproductivity into middle age, free from the responsibilities, the stresses, the hazards, and the trials of childbirth—but at a price.

Because of her biologic constitution and the vicissitudes of her environment, the woman enters the climacteric with uneasy and uncertain tread. It is a time of introspection, of inventorying, and of soul-searching; she analyzes her limitations, her frustrations, her secret sorrows. It is a period of boredom, of anxiety, of phobias and cancer fears, of waning romance. It is a period of emotional irritability, which appears at a stage in life when her nervous system is unstable and vulnerable and when her declining ovarian activity provokes a general glandular imbalance. Little wonder, then, that the psychosexual upheaval connected with this period brings with it a train of varied symptoms that one physician may stamp as psychoneurotic and another as menopausal.

The psychosomatic aspects of the menopause bring to mind a scene in Shakespeare's *Macbeth*, which lends substance to the concept that an emotional upheaval occurring during any given endocrine disorder is only an aggravation of pre-existing neurotic tendencies. It is quite probable that Lady Macbeth became severely ill only when the environmental stresses were piled upon existing biologic deviations at her period of life. Macbeth is questioning the doctor about his wife (V, 3):

> *Macb.* How does your patient, doctor?
> *Doct.* Not so sick, my lord,
> As she is troubled with thick-coming fancies
> That keep her from her rest.
> *Macb.* Cure her of that.
> Canst thou not minister to a mind diseas'd,
> Pluck from the memory a rooted sorrow,
> Raze out the written troubles of the brain,
> And with some sweet oblivious antidote
> Cleanse the stuff'd bosom of that perilous stuff
> Which weighs upon the heart?
> *Doct.* Therein the patient
> Must minister to himself.

Now, as then, some physicians harbor this Doctor's attitude that "therein the patient must minister to himself." Furthermore, many thunder denunciations on all who administer hormones for the relief of the climacteric, believing that it is a natural physiologic process. But, writes Dr. Minnie B. Goldberg of the University of California, "Why it should be more moral to treat the nervous symptoms of the menopause with barbiturates or tranquilizers than with natural substitutional products for a physiologic lack is a bit difficult to comprehend."

While it is true that the menopause is a physiologic process and represents a period of adjustment to a new hormonal *milieu intérieur,* why withhold measures that may make the transition smoother or prevent disabling pathologic processes, be they psychologic, neurologic or metabolic? The fact is that many women may be restored from chronic invalidism to mental and physical health with the judicious use of steroid hormone therapy. We, as physicians, have within our power the means both to diagnose and to alleviate the distressing symptoms of the menopause. Those prepared to receive the lessons of endocrinology may offer these weary-laden women the hope that much

Woman's Destiny

can be done for them, that their gloom may be dispersed and their sufferings alleviated. We may share something of the optimism of Browning's "Rabbi Ben Ezra:"

> Grow old along with me!
> The best is yet to be,
> The last of life, for which the first was made:
> Our times are in His hand
> Who saith "A whole I planned,
> Youth shows but half; trust God: see all,
>   nor be afraid!"

That life begins at forty is a cliche, we all know; but for the vestal virgins, freed at forty from their service in the temples of Rome, life did begin so tardily, in a sense. The climacteric need not be the end of fruitful experience: if life does not begin in it, neither need it end. But if the advancing years are to be good, we must not deny those who require hormonal therapy for the troubles that beset them towards the "last of life."

The difficulties of the menopause—the imbalance of the *autonomic nervous system*, the psychogenic disorders, the metabolic disturbances—continue, in mild to severe form, to the end of life. Many women cannot adjust to them; although their hormonal environment can be improved, they envision goals that must remain inaccessible. Their inner illuminations fade; their moments of exaltation give way to hours of melancholic gloom. In those who have staked everything on their femininity, the pathetic urgency to turn back the flight of time contributes to their crisis, for the life history and destiny of each woman are dependent to a great degree on the intensity and duration of her ovarian function. Of these matters Simone de Beauvoir has written well in her *The Second Sex*.

She who faces up to the responsibilities of her advancing years, who sets realistic goals, who minimizes her slights and hurts, real and imagined—she will grow old with grace and human worth. To her, the judicious use of hormones is of immeasurable help.

20

A Woman's Garment

The woman shall not wear that which pertaineth unto a man, neither shall a man put on a woman's garment: for all that do so are abomination unto the Lord thy God.

Deuteronomy 22:5

Is the behavior of males who yield to an irrespressible urge to dress in woman's clothing conditioned by environment or by glandular imbalance? A manifestation of distorted sexual values or of compulsion neurosis?

OUR SOCIETY TENDS to emasculate the modern male; one may read how in every Sunday's magazines. *Transvestism*, it is often said, is increasing, although any increase may be more apparent than real. For transvestism was something of a problem in Biblical days: Moses condemned it as an abomination to the Lord, castigated transvestites, and forbade them to "enter into the congregation of the Lord."

What another era regarded as willful sinfulness, and soundly denounced, a latter-day prophet of Israel, Sigmund Freud, dismissed as merely an abnormality of behavior that is obsessive. The inquiring eyes of modern science are taking another look at transvestism. To the theories that try to explain the motivations that grip men to cross-dress—environmental conditioning, glandular disorders, and psychic disturbances—has been added a fourth dimension: possible defects in the inherited chromosomal constitution.

Transvestism is a form of behavior in which a person has a compulsive desire to dress in the clothes of the opposite sex. When practiced in privacy, it is said to be a repressed and controlled addiction; when flaunted in public, it is regarded as abnormal. Many women dress in slacks and men's shirts purely for convenience; and, occasionally, men participate in amateur shows as female impersonators. Certainly, such single instances do not constitute transvestism, because they spring from no uncontrollable urge to gain erotic satisfaction. However, the male who repeatedly seeks such roles and, more particularly, the professional members of troupes are in many instances latent or true transvestites. In the past year, several dozen companies of female impersonators toured the nation's theaters and night clubs, playing to record audiences. What explanation can be offered for the increase in popularity of this form of entertainment? Of course, one recalls that in China and in Shakespeare's time men played all female roles for quite other reasons.

Havelock Ellis called this deviation "eonism," after the Chevalier d'Éon, famous French historical figure who was a transvestite. That unfortunate gentleman wrote with such excellence on history and political economy that he was sent on a diplomatic mission to Russia in 1755, where he dressed as a woman in order to win the confidence of the Empress. His disguise worked, and he secured a treaty favorable to France. Later, he held several high governmental positions and served as secretary to the French Ambassador to England, then as minister plenipotentiary. Wagers were placed that the Chevalier actually was a woman; but when he died, an autopsy revealed that he was undeniably a male. His name lives on; although d'Éon served his country faithfully, eonism has become synonymous with transvestism and a badge of dishonor.

Dr. Magnus Hirschfeld was first to use the term *transvestism*. It was his belief that the condition was an unusual sexual anomaly not necessarily related to homosexuality, and accordingly he recognized four types: heterosexual, homosexual, narcissistic, and asexual. On the other hand,

Search the Scriptures

Alfred Kinsey's investigations led him to assume that this sexual deviation is a psychologically conditioned inclination, acquired after birth as a result of precise and specific environmental experiences; he disputed the theories of glandular causation and constitutional origin.

Historic reference to men who, by choice, behaved like women has appeared often in widely dispersed civilizations. Thirty centuries ago, this aberration was linked with religious customs in the worship of certain Babylonian deities. And further west among the Phoenicians, the Galli were sexual deviants who consecrated themselves to the worship of Astarte, a goddess akin to the Venus of the early Greeks.

In another part of the world, the Aztecs, for religious purposes, deliberately encouraged the Mujerado, who lost his position in society as a man and assumed female clothing and manners, for the sole reward of the high honor of being a religious consecrate. So, too, among the ancient Hebrews 'consecrated ones,' who actually were deviants or effeminate men, dwelt near the temples. The First Book of Kings (14:22, 24) refers to them as sodomites:

> And Judah did evil in the sight of the Lord, and they provoked him to jealousy with their sins. . . .
> And there were also sodomites in the land: and they did according to all the abominations of the nations which the Lord cast out before the children of Israel.

In the original Hebrew, *kadesh*, literally 'holy one,' is the word which in translation was writ as 'sodomite'—not exactly a complimentary substitute. In the Christian liturgy the resounding passage, "Holy, holy, holy, is the Lord of hosts: The whole earth is full of his glory" (Isaiah 6:3), is quite a familiar one. In the Hebrew, the word for Holy is *kadosh*. This passage is recited solemnly beginning in the words 'Kadosh, kadosh, kadosh'—Holy, holy, holy. It is not difficult to surmise how the word kadesh evolved to describe someone set apart for holy purposes. In later years, this term was used to refer to 'devotees of the fertility

A Woman's Garment

cult.' Without this historic background, the association of the word kadosh (holy) with kadesh (sodomite) would appear wholly ludicrous. The reforming zeal of King Josiah ultimately prevailed and these abodes of immorality and heresy were destroyed (2 Kings 23:19).

In our own day, transvestism in the United States and Europe increases. If the reports are correct, the increase is a phenomenon that strikingly illustrates the force of psychologic conditioning. This undesirable by-product of our way of life is a reflection of the mores and manners of the society in which we live. Unhappily, cross-dressing is not an uncommon occurrence amongst highschool boys and girls, to whom it is known as "Hi-Drag." They form separate clubs where the "queens" (boys in female garments) and the "gays" (girls wearing male attire) gather for the sake of kinship and understanding. These frustrated children find happiness when they are with their own kind.

A few years ago, the newspapers carried the story of a scion of an aristocratic southern family, who was murdered in his hideaway shack in the country. When found, he was dressed in woman's garb. Beside his battered head was a woman's shoe with a steel-pointed heel, and on one foot was its mate.

Several years ago, Dr. Christian Hamburger of Denmark was the recipient of world-wide publicity when he transformed a male transvestite into a female by surgery and hormone administration. Since that time, many physicians interested in problems of sex have been besieged by requests from discontented individuals to be transformed to the opposite sex. Within a few years after his report, Dr. Hamburger received such requests from three hundred and thirty-seven men and one hundred and eight women. In a more recent treatise on this subject, Dr. Jean Vague of Marseilles writes that the abnormal desire for sex transformation is widespread and endemic. The persons in this category, he feels, are not necessarily active, but all are at least passive homosexuals. The compulsive desire for sex transformation is an ancient malady, he states, and afflicted individuals harbor the belief that, but for some error in development, they actually belong to the opposite sex.

One presumably intelligent college student, after studying the subject of chromosomes in his biology class, sought consultation with me requesting chromosome determinations. He earnestly believed that his was a female (XX) sex pattern, or at least a mixture of the male (XY) with the female (XX). This student argued that if such evidence could be brought forth, then his request for sex transformation would have valid support.

This young man's idea was ahead of his time; what he had surmised was prophetic. Only recently such a mosaic of XX/XY chromosomal sex patterns has been found in certain cases of defective sexual development. As our laws are constituted, sex transformation of normally developed individuals is illegal. However, the transformation of hermaphrodites and pseudo-hermaphrodites into the sex consonant with their psychic and emotional drives has been performed satisfactorily and within the bounds of legality.

With the American soldier who was the subject of much notoriety, Dr. Hamburger partially succeeded by castration and by the administration of female hormones. Though some degree of breast development may be induced and the pitch of the voice may be altered somewhat, the beard growth and the need for shaving cannot be eliminated except by meticulous electrolysis. Whether this deluded male is now happier in feminine guise as a "female" performer and entertainer remains a secret.

What should be the attitude of society, of the legal profession, of the psychiatrist, and of the endocrinologist toward the transvestite with his compulsion for sex transformation? In quest for an answer, one may turn to the scriptures and find a partial answer:

> He that is wounded in the stones ... shall not enter into the congregation of the Lord. Deuteronomy 23:1

A Woman's Garment

In our enlightened age, should medical assistance ever be denied a transvestite? Therapy, psychiatric or endocrinologic, is difficult and, often, futile; nor is sex transformation through surgery a good answer to the problem. A part of the answer is early awareness, for as Milton wrote in *Paradise Regained:* "The childhood shows the man, / As morning shows the day," and as Wordsworth repeated after him: "The child is father of the man."

Yet attentive parents often observe peculiar behavior in their child or children, only then to conceal or to ignore it. They should not ignore tendencies to cross-dress, but seek help at once. For with proper guidance, and with conditioning before the tendency becomes the habit, much may be accomplished for this serious problem of behavior.

21

Sins Be As Scarlet

Come now, and let us reason together, saith the Lord: though your sins be as scarlet, they shall be as white as snow; though they be red like crimson, they shall be as wool. Isaiah 1:18

> Why, from antiquity until today, is sin red, crimson, scarlet?

THE OLD AND NEW TESTAMENTS provide passages that equate shades of red with sinfulness. Isaiah refers to sins as *scarlet* and *red like crimson*. The repetition of a word-image—and the Old Testament abounds in it—is used by the prophet not only for effect but for emphasis. In mystical language, the New Testament prophet, John, dramatically reinforced the notion that sin wears a color. He, too, warned the people in his Book of Revelation (17:1-4) of:

> ... the great whore that sitteth upon many waters;
> With whom the kings of the earth have committed fornication, and the inhabitants of the earth have been made drunk with the wine of her fornication.
> ... and I saw a woman sit upon a scarlet-coloured beast, full of names of blasphemy, ...
> And the woman was arrayed in purple and scarlet colour. ...

It is fascinating to examine the use of red shades to denote sin: vivid design in time's tapestry. Nathaniel Hawthorne's *The Scarlet Letter* tells the tragic story of Hester, a young woman who suffered the indignity of being branded with a scarlet "A"—the letter that marked her an adulteress. The "scarlet woman," the "red light district,"

Sins Be As Scarlet

"her crimson past" connote fully the relation of vivid red to sin, although ruby lips and rouged cheeks are today used with impunity not only to embellish but to attract, and the promise of feminine glamour not infrequently serves as a want ad.

Poets and artists have depended on red and its various shades to express sin; numerous paintings of debauchery have females either scarlet-garbed or red-haired. Read the passages of Shakespeare's *The Rape of Lucrece* (lines 475-483) and give thought to the allusion subtly created when "lust-breathed Tarquin" is asked by the unwilling victim of his desire:

> But she with vehement prayers urgeth still
> Under what colour he commits this ill.
> Thus he replies: 'The colour in thy face,
> That even for anger makes the lily pale
> And the red rose blush at her own disgrace,
> Shall plead for me and tell my loving tale.
> Under that colour am I come to scale
>   Thy never-conquer'd fort: the fault is thine,
>   For those thine eyes betray thee unto mine.'

The question remains: why should red, but not green or blue or yellow, be equated with sex and moral turpitude? The eye is drawn to other hues, but only a red is coupled with sin. Green is a reminder of earth's rebirth in the spring, and implies hope; gold indicates warmth and richness; the sky and ocean are blue to the eye, and suggest harmony. In nature, there is a minimum of red except for fruit, flowers, fire, and fall's spent leaves. And even though white is thought correct for a bridal gown, again history reports that red once was popular. The custom was not lasting because, in the human mind is ingrained a feeling that white expresses purity and virginity while red does not.

Why red's wicked reputation among colors? The Old Testament tells us that man's downfall, and what is termed "original sin," took place in the Garden of Eden; Adam and Eve were cast from Paradise because they disobeyed

God and ate of the forbidden fruit, generally accepted as a red apple. The paintings of such masters as Titian and Rubens display this red fruit; the apple, although not specified in Genesis, became the fruit of temptation. Milton named it, in *Paradise Lost*, as "fair apples," described previously in the poem as "ruddy and gold." Plainly, the fruit's color did not cause it to be attached to evil; instead, it was probably selected because a "sinful shade" emphasized a sinful deed, and the apple suited all requirements.

Another theory concerns the shedding of blood during sacrifice, with which pagans sought to appease their gods and which the Ancient Hebrews practiced to win Jehovah's forgiveness of sins. Sacrifice was a ritual, and the Hebrews felt that their sins were shed from them as an animal's blood drained away after the slaughtering; an unblemished red heifer was their special offering. Christians find their answer in Christ's blood, which was offered, during the crucifixion, as the supreme sacrifice for the atonement of all men's sins. By its blood offering, the sacrifice has a relation, direct or indirect, to sin.

A Biblical verse, like any remark taken out of context, may invite misunderstanding. But Isaiah's words regarding sin follow seventeen verses of condemnation of his people. Judah had many vices, yet Isaiah seemed most wrathful toward the nation's lack of sexual morality and rebuked them, saying:

> Ah sinful nation, a people laden with iniquity, a seed of evildoers, children that are corrupters: . . .
> Except the Lord of hosts had left unto us a very small remnant, we should have been as Sodom, and we should have been like unto Gomorrah.
> Hear the word of the Lord, ye rulers of Sodom: give ear unto the law of our God, ye people of Gomorrah.
> . . . your hands are full of blood.
> How is the faithful city become an harlot! . . .
>
> 1:4, 9, 10, 15, 21

Sins Be As Scarlet

The great prophet gave particular attention to sins of the flesh in these verses. He selected scarlet, red, and crimson as symbolic of immorality, warning that his people had been spared the fate of Sodom because only "a very small remnant" refrained from the corruption that brought its destruction. Sin's color was thus defined and eloquently expressed by Isaiah, in the eighth century B.C.

The identification of sin with red could date back to times much earlier than Isaiah's: the Mosaic laws proclaim a menstruating woman unclean and sexual intercourse during menstruation sinful. It is possible that the symbolism of red can be traced back to an even earlier period. Our oldest civilizations flourished in India, where the macaque (a short-tailed monkey) is indigenous, and not infrequently revered. The sexual habits of the macaque were in all probability closely observed. Perhaps it is in the study of the sex skin changes in these primates that an answer to the question may be found. At the time when the ovary prepares to extrude the ovum or egg, the genital zone of the macaque becomes turgid and takes on a brilliant red color. The period of greatest sexual receptivity in the female macaque is reached during this period of turgescence and "redness" of the sex skin. Flaunting her nakedness, she sports her colors; her "redness" is her open invitation to mating.

Such terms as "red light" and "the scarlet woman" are profoundly symbolic because vestiges of our most primitive impulses crop up from time to time. As man evolved, these blatant advertisements, veritable neon signs, were no longer necessary to the highest species, man being moved by more subtle appeals. In the phylogenetic development of man, the female homo sapiens apparently lost the readily visible color changes of the sex skin inherent in the macaque. Yet today, the eyes of science have discovered that indeed woman has retained significant color changes of the perineum. Greatly modified, the sex skin of the adult female still retains the atavistic red. In the study of *gyneco-*

logic disorders and during pregnancy, colors of the genitalia, varying from vivid red to purple, can be made visible by illumination with an ultraviolet light.

In the light of all of these considerations, we should not be surprised that sex, sin and scarlet have been interwoven in the fabric of our literature and mores. It was no mere accident that Isaiah observed: "though your sins be as scarlet, . . . though they be red like crimson. . . ."

22

No Breasts Hath She

We have a little sister, and she hath no breasts: what shall we do for our sister in the day when she shall be spoken for?
If she be a wall, we will build upon her a palace of silver: and if she be a door, we will enclose her with boards of cedar.
The Song of Solomon 8:8-9

> *Is the little sister's condition less a handicap today, or more? Are our walls stouter, our doors more open?*

BLESS ME, Socrates said, looking around in the market where all that any Athenian wanted lay piled in profusion, "what a lot of things a man can do without." One of the things that we of this culture can *not* do without is, apparently, the female breast.

We are a nation of breast-worshippers. In art and literature, in the theater and the movies, on television and in advertising, we glorify the female mammary glands. For a woman, the full development of her bosom is a needful thing. She knows that men consider well-formed breasts the mark of beauty and of womanhood, and even equate them, erroneously, with sexual prowess. In our day, we have seen a great resurgence of the esteem of the female breast as symbol of sex, femininity, and abundance.

Yet has it not been so always? With and without the singing of birds and the voice of the turtle dove in the land, poets have sung with more charm, perhaps, than innocence:

Thy two breasts are like two young roes that are twins, which feed among the lilies.

> Until the day break, and the shadows flee away, I will get me to the mountain of myrrh, and to the hill of frankincense.
> The Song of Solomon 4:5-6

Adequate maturation of the breasts was an important factor in the marriage marts. Small wonder, then, that the brothers of the little sister were worried. One must feel the urgency of their question: "what shall we do for our sister in the day when she shall be spoken for?"

Was the sister suffering from sexual infantilism or merely from the absence of the growth of her breasts? How were her brothers to meet the competition in the market place? Her lack had perhaps given her such feelings of inferiority that she had become asocial, introverted, unapproachable: an impenetrable wall. If so, her brothers would endow her handsomely, would "build upon her a palace of silver." On the other hand, if in order to compensate for her wants and to prove her femininity she had become too approachable, even promiscuous—a hospitable door through which all could enter—they would chaperone and confine her, would "enclose her with boards of cedar."

This interpretation of what probably beset the little sister and her brothers followed my study of two young women with sexual infantilism whom I saw in consultation. The first was twenty-three years old, shy and retiring; because she was ashamed of her nakedness, she had refused an offer of marriage. Substitutional therapy, with cyclic use of estrogens over a two-year period, changed her personality to that of an outgoing person and resolved her problem. She is happily married and is most appreciative of hormone therapy, which she has continued.

The second young woman, of about the same age, was bold and brazen; her every action was an effort to show how womanly she could be. I was scandalized to find her trademark tatooed on the base of what we may call, I suppose, her escutcheon: "Pay as you enter." Hers, surely, was a device of over-compensation.

Lack of breast development may derive from one of

three causes: delayed pubescence, *ovarian* failure, or target-gland failure—failure of the breasts to respond to the hormones produced by the ovaries, the estrogens. For delayed pubescence, time and expectant waiting are all that is necessary, although breast maturation may be hastened by the administration of hormones; and such hastening is valuable where anxiety may lead to psychic problems. For ovarian failure, the cyclic administration of estrogens will result, usually, in excellent breast growth. For target gland failure, often encountered, the addition of hormones usually proves, unfortunately, valueless. Because the breast tissues fail to respond to the stimulus of endogenous hormones, they also fail to respond, in almost all cases, to exogenous hormones. One may speculate into which one of the three categories the "little sister" falls, in the Song of Solomon.

Archaeologists continue to unearth statues from ancient civilizations that depict women with voluptuous breasts. In the ancient cultures of India, Egypt, and Babylon, prominent breasts were accepted for what they appeared to be, an erotic fixture. Women in all periods of our civilization have been conscious of the well-developed bosom. The ancient Jews had an appreciation of the breasts that was closer to hearth and home—earthy as it was. Proverbs exhorts a husband to:

> ... rejoice with the wife of thy youth.
> Let her be as the loving hind and pleasant roe; let her breasts satisfy thee at all times; and be thou ravished always with her love.   Proverbs 5:18-19

Nor was the life-giving sustenance furnished by the lactating breast disregarded. Ashley Montagu believes that the Psalmist, in unconscious reverberation, almost certainly had this in mind when he wrote the words, "I lift up mine eyes unto the hills, from whence cometh my sustenance."

But in Solomon's Song the human breast is glorified. In eight short chapters the subject is sung eight times without sham or shame.

> A bundle of myrrh is my well-beloved unto me; he shall lie all night betwixt my breasts.   Song of Solomon 1:13

The Song has been termed by some as pagan and lewd. Such pious disapproval of a theme written with delicacy and tenderness nearly resulted in exclusion of this classic of religious literature from the Bible. Even at the close of the nineteenth century, the Reverend E. P. Eddruff, Prebendary of Salisbury Cathedral, admonished that "such a book as the Song of Solomon may not be fitted for public reading in a mixed congregation, or even in private reading by the impure of heart." Despite such protestations, the Song will always remain a paean to love, in praise of the body beautiful, and a timeless tribute to womanhood.

Nor was it very different in Imperial Rome when Aulus Gellius said:

> And do you suppose that nature has given bosoms to women only to add to their beauty—more for the sake of ornament than for the purpose of nourishing children? Because some women believe this, they unnaturally endeavor to dry up and extinguish that sacred fountain of the body, the natural nourishment of man, with great hazard, turning and corrupting the channel of their milk, lest it should render the distinction of their beauty less marked.

What a familiar bell is rung by this commentary written in the second century. *Nihil novum est.*

The veneration of the female breast is nothing new. Man has always been enthralled, it seems, by the sight of the shapely breast. Women throughout history have been aware of the allure to men of reticent exposure of the subtly clothed breast. The plunging neckline may not be equated with plunging morals, but certainly it is an integral part of a coquettish pattern, of flirtation, of invitation to attention. The extent to which a woman is willing to reveal, or to emphasize, her breasts is also a measure of her conscious sexuality. While there is no sexual symbolism in the nakedly displayed bosom of the native African woman, there is considerable sexual identification with the purposefully low-cut revealing gown of the fully clothed woman. The young matron or teen-ager with a tightly fitting sweater covering an uplift bra is merely exaggerating her desirability and sometimes her availability. Feminine curves have been appreciated since Adam beheld Eve. In an inconstant world of continuous and spectacular change, one thing remains constant, and that is the unchanging appreciation by civilized man of the bosom as a symbol of fertility, bounty and beauty.

23

Thy Faith Can Make Thee Whole

And a woman having an issue of blood twelve years, which had spent all her living upon physicians, neither could be healed of any,
Came behind him, and touched the border of his garment: and immediately her issue of blood stanched.   Luke 8:43, 44

> *Was the woman with "an issue of blood" suffering from a psychosomatic disorder? And was she healed by faith?*

THE RELATIONSHIP between psychic and physical expression of human behavior lies in the realm of body and soul. Here mystery and illness are joined, and the cure of sickness takes many forms. The laying on of hands, an accepted form of therapy in early Christian times, was revived in England during the reign of Edward the Confessor; and Charles II later set aside one day each year to touch those afflicted with scrofula, "the King's disease." The throngs came to London; the King touched; and those who remained ill "lacked faith."

Yet faith can cure. The crutches that line the walls of the shrine at Sainte Anne de Beaupré, in Montmorency, Canada, bear witness to the cures rendered by faith. That multitudes journey from all the countries of the earth to the shrine of Lourdes, in France, means that some are healed, else the procession of suppliants would cease.

Two thousand years ago, the Holy Land was overrun by the Roman conquerors. A stubborn and stiffnecked people, the Hebrews suffered in silence heavy taxes and severe restrictions. Powerless to overthrow their oppressive yoke, they were frustrated and soul-sick. Although as they yearned for salvation they gave lip-service to Rome, their loyalty was to God, King of the Universe. It is not unnatural that during the ministry of Jesus of Nazareth, when the atmosphere was charged with peaceful disobedience, illness abounded, both organic and psychosomatic. Conversion neurosis of one type or another, frequent today, was perhaps more frequent then.

Today we readily accept the fact that many cases of migraine headaches, of mucous diarrhea, of hives, rashes and welts, and of localized spotty loss of head hair and even of all body hair, are physical manifestations of some deep-rooted emotional conflict; that is, that they are psychosomatic. Functional uterine bleeding, though readily explained as a disturbance of pituitary-ovarian balance, is nevertheless frequently emotional or psychogenic, a psychosomatic disorder; prolonged bleeding often follows severe fright or calamity. Psychosomatic disturbances play a role in uterine bleeding greater than that we have been wont to credit.

An inkling of such is suggested by the woman cured when she touched Jesus' garment. To her, He said: "Daughter, be of good comfort: thy faith hath made thee whole; go in peace." His ability to suffuse her being with such faith is a miracle that transcends the miracle of the arrest of bleeding within a few hours by today's potent hormonal preparations, such as *progesterone*. But even with these, the physician may cure, or he may add insult to injury. For if he wants confidence in his medication or his ability, if he neglects rapport with his patient, he may become an *iatrogenic* agent, just as certain pharmaceutical drugs may induce or compound a disease state, and thereby encourage his patients to develop hostility to the entire medical profession.

Mark, telling the same story that Luke told, bluntly took to task the doctors of his day when he described the woman as "having suffered many things at the hands of many physicians." Clearly, he implied that she suffered at their hands many more things than need be.

Human relationships, particularly those between doctor and patient, enter every medical situation. Like the lower animals, man fears and frets; unlike them, he has intellect and conscience, suffers forebodings and frightful imaginings, fluctuates in his emotional responses, and holds a wavering grasp on security. In one so sensitive occur reverberations that react on soma and psyche, body and soul; hence psychologic factors may as easily create as ameliorate a climate of preoccupation with infirmity. Therefore, the physician cannot study man in the biologic sense alone, for man's soul must be so nurtured that his body may function harmoniously in all its parts. The higher centers of the brain temper the activity of the pituitary glands, and the endocrines respond to the nervous system.

All of medicine is in part psychosomatic, for emotional factors influence physical behavior. The anxious suspicious person often suffers from dyspepsia; he "thinks" with his stomach. In the light of this concept, we may appreciate obesities in maladjusted persons, *exophthalmic goiter* in those subjected to repeated psychic trauma, menstrual disorders in women who experience stressful episodes, and *anorexia nervosa* in tormented young women. As Shakespear's King Lear observed (II, 4):

> we are not ourselves
> When nature, being oppress'd, commands the mind
> To suffer with the body.

Perhaps psychotherapy, faith healing, and the frequent beneficial effects that follow inadequate or inert therapy may take on new significance for us. Just as sorrow and pain may cause illness, and happiness and pleasure make for good health, so healing and cure do not come always from skill or from specifics. Faith, hope and charity ("but the greatest of these . . .") in an infusion of lovingkindness may do much more. Charity is the expression of righteousness,

Thy Faith Can Make Thee Whole

the obligation of the good man, man's act of reverence for man and of compassionate respect for him. Charity is the expression of a noble soul.

And charity is a great healer. In the management of illness that links psyche and soma, the general practitioner and specialist, the endocrinologist and psychiatrist, the psychotherapist and the minister meet on common ground. Christ spoke an eternal truth when he told the woman: "thy faith hath made thee whole; go in peace."

24

When Desire Shall Fail

Now king David was old and stricken in years; and they covered him with clothes, but he gat no heat.   1 Kings 1:1

> *Was the aging King David fairly tested? Did the struggle within him of righteousness against lust, and worse, abet his aging?*

FROM THE AGE OF FIFTY King David had no rest from misfortune and emotional turmoil. At seventy, he was so spent that he could lead his people no longer. Was he suffering from circulatory failure, severe *anemia*, *hypothyroidism*, or from general apathy and decrepitude? Rumblings were abroad, rumor raced through the kingdom that the King was through, and a Pretender laid claim to the throne.

The criteria that determined the King's loss of usefulness to his state seem strange to us. Was the fact that he "gat no heat" when covered with clothes a valid test of his fitness for leadership? The clinical observation was not strong enough to force his abdication; a more exacting test was needed; and the Israelites were prone to equate sexual prowess with virility and strength.

Wherefore his servants said unto him, Let there be sought for my lord the king a young virgin: and let her stand before the king, and let her cherish him, and let her lie in thy bosom, that my lord the king may get heat.

So they sought for a fair damsel throughout all the coasts of Israel, and found Abishag a Shunammite, and brought her to the king.

When Desire Shall Fail

And the damsel was very fair, and cherished the king, and ministered to him: but the king knew her not.   1 Kings 1:2-4

O! what pride must have been in the hearts of Abishag's parents when their daughter was chosen from all Israel to lie with the King. Although the origin of this sanctioned privilege is lost in antiquity, the claim of a prince continued through the middle ages. *Le droit du seigneur* could not be denied the lord of a domain, a baron, or the prince of a petty principality. The custom was extended to rights on the wedding night of the bride, and *droit de noce* was exacted from a subjugated people.

When Abishag tried to arouse the King, he still "gat no heat" and so failed the test. One can imagine her proud and anxious parents awaiting her return, their meeting, and the disillusion and dismay of all three. Word of the King's loss of virility spread throughout the kingdom, and his leadership was in doubt. Bath-sheba confronted the King to ensure that he declare her son by him, Solomon, as successor. And Solomon grew from strength to strength, and it is said of him that he had a thousand wives.

We may wonder whether David was in the throes of the *male climacteric*, akin to the female change of life. Although students of glandular physiology have not been unanimous that the male climacteric exists, proof that it does is strong. We know today that the climacteric occurs in both sexes, but that it affects only a small proportion of men. With advancing years, the endocrine output lessens to insufficiency. Testicular decline is great in some, less in others. But the activity of the adrenals persists at moderately normal levels in all; and when adrenal activity is greater than testicular, then *catabolism* overbalances *anabolism*, and decline follows inevitably.

Environmental and emotional factors play important roles in and can hasten senescence. An early indication is loss of virility or potentia. Prominent symptoms are psychosexual upheaval, insomnia, loss of concentration, irritability and melancholia. At this stage, men often become anti-social, and many lose confidence in their abilities. When psychogenic factors do not greatly overshadow the declining hormonal function of the testes, augmentive therapy, with androgens, has been most helpful in decreasing physical and mental fatigability, restoring vitality, and markedly improving general well-being.

None will dispute David's greatness as a king. When a lad, he was gifted in playing the lyre; he exhibited unusual courage as a humble shepherd who slew both lion and bear to protect his father's flocks. A favorite story describes his skill and bravery in killing Goliath, the giant, whom he faced alone, armed with only a slingshot. His sweet songs soothed the ill King Saul, who was to become obsessed by jealousy of him. Later, David was crowned king over the house of Judah; but after a long and hard-fought civil war waged against Saul's house, he emerged triumphant to reign over all Israel. His armies succeeded in conquering a feared and hated foe, the Philistines. Displaying adeptness in every way, he was a shrewd military leader, organizer and administrator. His nature was complex—a common denominator of most geniuses. He affords us a study in personality contrasts: humble but majestic; a sensitive psalmist yet a courageous warrior.

But King David had problems born of the struggle within him of opposing instincts. He was a man who cherished a specially close contact with God; from his simple faith had grown a strong, unbending conscience. And he was a man of great passion as well, having taken under the law, which also permitted him ten concubines, a number of wives. Within him, his conscience was now to struggle with his passion become lust, and worse.

At fifty, he succumbed to a temptation that was to bring sore trouble. At this age, we realize, a man may be tempted to prove his virility simply because he has less of it, because his sexuality has diminished. It is a time of life when physical, mental, and emotional upsets are not endured easily.

When Desire Shall Fail

Resistance is low; a surge of restlessness, of loneliness, is a constant threat. David had returned to his palace, after numerous victories, for relaxation well-earned. Restive, he

> arose from off his bed, and walked upon the roof of the king's house: and from the roof he saw a woman washing herself; and the woman was very beautiful to look upon.

She was Bath-sheba, wife of Uriah, one of David's brave and loyal captains.

A sudden desire subdued David's sense of righteousness. Impulsively, he sent for her, doubtlessly flattered to be summoned by her king. When she discovered herself pregnant, David lost no time in bringing her husband home from the battle, expecting, thereby, to conceal his adultery. But Uriah, despite all persuasion, refused to enter his house while Israel's army suffered on the grim field of battle. Sending Uriah back to the fighting, David had him placed in a position where death was inescapable, and, after the days of mourning, he took Bath-sheba to be his wife.

The effect of this tragic affair on a sensitive, God-loving man who had sought to live in righteousness cannot be overestimated. David had lost contact with his Lord, and no longer understood himself. Men of his character are prone to expect trouble; they even invite it as penance to soothe their feelings of guilt.

And trouble came, announced by Nathan the prophet:

> Wherefore hast thou despised the commandment of the Lord, to do evil in his sight? thou hast killed Uriah the Hittite with the sword, and hast taken his wife to be thy wife, . . .
> Now therefore the sword shall never depart from thine house; . . .
> Thus saith the Lord, Behold, I will raise up evil against thee.
> 2 Samuel 12:9-11

David had expected grim punishment, and Nathan's unstill voice foreshadowed his soul's agony. He suffered one misfortune after another, and his personal concerns gave him harsher trial than many overwhelming national problems. Certain that his woes were a sure sign of God's wrath, the once-majestic king aged beyond his years. As his feelings of guilt played havoc with his wellbeing, so he evidenced signs and symptoms of the male climacteric. The sight of Abishag surely stirred in him old memories; but she could not arouse him, and he failed the test.

A man's strength comes from proper endocrine functioning and peace of mind. Because Israel required a strong king, it accepted as the symptom of infirmity a lack of sexual desire. Yet no yardstick has been devised that equates a man's age with his ability properly to grapple with his duties and responsibility, whether of state, profession, or business. The test of the ancient Hebrews, however exacting, was and is too fallible.

25

Seven Ages

Remember now thy Creator in the days of thy youth, while the evil days come not, nor the years draw nigh, when thou shalt say, I have no pleasure in them;
While the sun, or the light, or the moon, or the stars, be not darkened, nor the clouds return after the rain:
In the day when the keepers of the house shall tremble, and the strong men shall bow themselves, and the grinders cease because they are few, and those that look out of the windows be darkened,
And the doors shall be shut in the streets, when the sound of the grinding is low, and he shall rise up at the voice of the bird, and all the daughters of musick shall be brought low;
Also when they shall be afraid of that which is high, and fears shall be in the way, and the almond-tree shall flourish, and the grasshopper shall be a burden, and desire shall fail: . . .
Or ever the silver cord be loosed, or the golden bowl be broken, or the pitcher be broken at the fountain, or the wheel broken at the cistern.
Then shall the dust return to the earth as it was: and the spirit shall return unto God who gave it.
Vanity of vanities, saith the preacher; all is vanity.
Ecclesiastes 12:1-8

> *Has the stress of our times, the way of our lives, aged man? Towards the aged, what should society's attitude be?*

MAN ATTAINED UNBELIEVABLE AGE in the antidiluvian era: Methuselah lived 969 years, Noah 950. The life-span in the postdiluvian era is comparable to our own: Moses died at 120, and King David lived out three score years and ten. What has happened to the "nucleic acid moiety," or to the aging process, that has brought about this radical change? Was it a change in the nature of the foodstuffs that sustained man, or new unaccustomed viruses that afflicted him? Or was it—let us remember that the priest Berossos, writing in Babylonia in the third century B.C., totalled the reigns of three pre-flood kings at 68,400 years—that the Biblical "year" was much shorter than ours, or that the geneaologies were composed before man had developed an exact chronology and felt the need to measure time with precision?

At the beginning of the eighteenth century, the average life-span in the civilized world, although many reached a ripe old age, was not more than thirty-five years, and at the beginning of the twentieth century, in the United States, was only forty-nine years. Today, it is seventy-two years. The "three score and ten" of Biblical promise has become a reality for more people now than ever before. Whereas only four per cent of our population reached the age of sixty in 1900, more than nine per cent are sixty five or older today.

The process of aging, in all probability, has ever been the same. Centuries apart, two poet-philosophers, Koheleth-Ecclesiastes and Shakespeare, described advancing age after the same fashion. To compare the style of Ecclesiastes, cloaked in mystery of language and metaphor, with the style of Shakespeare, clearer to us and relatively simpler, some eighteen centuries later is fascinating. In *The Comedy of Errors* (V, 1), Aegeon remarks the attrition of his aging:

> Though now this grained face of mine be hid
> In sap-consuming winter's drizzled snow,
> And all the conduits of my blood froze up,
> Yet hath my night of life some memory,
> My wasting lamps some fading glimmer left,
> My dull deaf ears a little use to hear. . . .

In the more sophisticated *As You Like It* (II, 7) the caustic, melancholy Jacques sets forth the human condition:

Seven Ages

> All the world's a stage,
> And all the men and women merely players:
> They have their exits and their entrances;
> And one man in his time plays many parts,
> His acts being seven ages....

Then he describes each age in turn—the infant "Mewling and puking in the nurse's arms;" the boy "creeping like snail / Unwillingly to school;" the lover, "Sighing like a furnace;" the soldier / "Seeking the bubble reputation / Even in the cannon's mouth;" the justice / "In fair round belly with good capon lin'd,"...

> The sixth age shifts
> Into the lean and slipper'd pantaloon,
> With spectacles on nose and pouch on side,
> His youthful hose, well sav'd, a world too wide
> For his shrunk shank; and his big manly voice,
> Turning again toward childish treble, pipes
> And whistles in his sound. Last scene of all,
> That ends this strange eventful history,
> Is second childishness and mere oblivion,
> Sans teeth, sans eyes, sans taste, sans everything.

The aging process is universal. As the perceptive Shakespeare captured it for his lively audiences, he seems to have paraphrased many of the thoughts and the symbols of Koheleth-Ecclesiastes:

"the grinders cease because they are few" *sans teeth*
"those that look out of the windows be darkened" *sans eyes*
"sound of the grinding is low" *my dull deaf ears*
"the daughters of musick shall be brought low" *childish treble*
"almond tree shall flourish" *face of mine be hid in snow*
"desire shall fail" *night of life some memory*
"wheel broken at the cistern" *conduits of my blood froze up*

For many centuries scholars have sought to unravel the mystery of Koheleth's description of that time of man's sojourn on earth when his life ceases to be a joy, when his faculties decline and his strength fails. Koheleth wrote of the aged with compassion, and in the twelfth chapter he has given us a remarkable exposition of the rigors of aging and of its inevitable toll. In so doing, he touched on several medical fields, of which we believe little was known. Linking antiquity to the present, his observations are pertinent:

"The clouds return after the rain." Here the poet-clinician recognizes the mental and emotional changes associated with aging: depression, disappointment, dreary expectations.

"The keepers of the house shall tremble." Variously interpreted, this metaphor may refer to trembling hands or to the jerky, gasping heaving of the chest, which houses the vital organs.

"And the strong men shall bow themselves." The muscles, cartilage and bones degenerate, the legs bow, the shoulders stoop, perhaps with arthritis.

"And he shall rise up at the voice of the bird." Almost all old people wake and arise early in the morning.

"They shall be afraid of that which is high, and fears shall be in the way." Fear, particularly of heights, and apprehension often accompany the infirmities of old age.

"Or ever the silver cord be loosed, or the golden bowl be broken." In keeping with the anatomical allegory so precisely drawn, the silver cord becomes the spinal column, weakened by the demineralization of the bones (osteoporosis); and the broken bowl denotes the deterioration, through hemorrhage or softening, of the brain in its cranial vault.

"The pitcher broken at the fountain." The broken pitcher denotes the urinary incontinence and the troublesome prostate gland common in aged men.

"The wheel broken at the cistern." Here is a graphic metaphor for cardiac failure: the heart pump is affected by coronary thrombosis.

What is aging? It is the wear and tear of tissues throughout the body. The process starts, actually, with one's first breath, surely with the first lusty cry at birth. Building processes predominate from birth until late puberty; then, for a varying number of years, the forces that build (anabolism) and those that destroy (catabolism) reach some sort of equilibrium, before the rigors of aging begin. Insulin

Seven Ages

and growth and gonadal hormones contribute to anabolism, and certain hormones of the adrenal contribute to catabolism. When the anabolic gonadal function (ovarian or testicular) declines, breakdown of tissue proceeds at a more rapid rate than build-up. As aging depends on the hormonal chemistry of the body, so it depends on genetic endowment, also.

Sex desire in healthy persons parallels gonadal function; hence the allusion in Ecclesiastes is in accord with physiological principles. Shakespeare's Poins makes the point more graphically and realistically: "Is it not strange that desire should so many years outlive performance?" (II Henry IV, II, 4). Lack of sexual performance is indeed one of the indices that aging is upon us.

Yet the calendar is a poor index of a person's age. Too often persons are forced to retire while still mentally and physically alert, and in many of them, their stimulation and self-confidence taken away, their will to live ebbs, and they die before their time. Countless "old" people, even with physical limitations, live vibrant useful lives—meeting the challenges of each day, maintaining their interests and talents, living one day at a time, without regrets for yesterday's mistakes or anxieties about tomorrow's: "for the morrow shall take thought for the things of itself." In many, facing the sunset of their existence, the spark of youth persists; they prove the fallacy of judging competence by a fixed scale of years.

Society is the beneficiary of untold wealth bequeathed to it by men considered long past their prime, as Longfellow makes clear in his "Morituri Salutamus":

> It is too late! Ah, nothing is too late
> Till the tired heart shall cease to palpitate.
> Cato learned Greek at eighty; Sophocles
> Wrote his grand *Oedipus*, and Simonides
> Bore off the prize of verse from his compeers,
> When each had numbered more than four-score years, . . .
> Chaucer, at Woodstock with the nightingales,

> At sixty wrote the *Canterbury Tales;*
> Goethe at Weimar, toiling to the last,
> Completed *Faust* when eighty years were past.
> These are indeed exceptions; but they show
> How far the gulf-stream of our youth may flow
> Into the arctic regions of our lives. . . .
> For age is opportunity no less
> Than youth itself, though in another dress, . . .

What of the attitude of modern society toward the aged? Is it one of responsible acceptance, of wise understanding, of social usefulness? Or is it evasive, disrespectful, socially destructive?

The scientific aspects of aging receive more attention than ever before, and the social, political and economic problems of the aged population currently are in the national forum, especially medical care for the aged. Inasmuch as the population of senior citizens is expanding phenomenally, our society must shape its resources to meet and to ameliorate their plight. While the increase in population is owing to the great advances in the medical and biological sciences during the past century, solutions to the problems that the increase creates must involve not only expanding medical care but also attending a matrix of social, economic, and environmental facts.

Aged human beings have fundamentally the same problems around the world. They require the same commodities: food, shelter, clothing. But, in whatever culture, they also require another kind of sustenance—as Dr. David Sherman, President of the American Geriatric Society, has stated, "emotional sustenance and self-esteem."

> How dull it is to pause, to make an end,
> To rust unburnished, not to shine in use!

saith the poet. To be active usefully and responsibly, to be wanted and valued—these are the best tonics for the boredom and the frustration of old age in our society.

Seven Ages

In one way or another, the problem of the aged belongs to each individual: the aged are genuinely ours, as we must some day be numbered of them. We must create opportunities for their work and their play, for their answering a need that bestows on them, whether dependent or independent, a sense of worth and of belonging.

"Honor thy father and thy mother that thy days may be long upon the land which the Lord thy God giveth thee." Do we enough remember this Commandment, or has our commitment to it passed with our unfaith in the old gods? Are we too willing to hand over to another—to a social agency, a "fund," a hospital, "the Government"—responsibilities that properly are our own? We are society, and society cannot avoid or shun the problem of the aged; meeting it will require our best attitudes and understanding.

Old age should not mark merely the end of living; it should be instead the season to harvest the fruits of a full life, years of maturity and wisdom and of their rewards. Many elderly persons have special contributions to make to society; their opportunities should not be denied them. Unfortunately, too many men and women of good faculty are put out to pasture, like a "well-run steed," when their mature judgment and experience could be used to serve the common good.

"Teach us to number our days . . ." (Psalms 90:12)—so that each of us will put away something enduring for our old age, complete a work undone, enjoy a useful hobby, serve the community, conserve material acquisitions for security. The self-respect and the dignity of the aged must be preserved. Tennyson aptly expressed in "Ulysses" what seems to be lacking in our times—a much needed reassessment of our attitude toward the aged—their aspirations, and the obligations of the family unit, of society at large and, not the least, of our government.

> Old age hath yet his honor and his toil;
> Death closes all; but something ere the end,
> Some work of noble note, may yet be done.

26

Hewers of Flesh and Drawers of Water

Honour a physician with the honour due him . . . for the Lord hath created him.
For of the Most High cometh healing, and he shall receive honour of the king.
The skill of the physician shall lift up his head: and in the sight of great men he shall be in admiration.
Ecclesiasticus 38:1-3

Whence Medicine? Whither? Have its specialties helped or harmed its practice?

THE ART OF HEALING is a natural craft conceived in sympathy and born of necessity. The earliest medicine men were, as some still may be, magicians, sorcerers, and witch doctors. Yet during Egypt's zenith, three thousand years ago, medicine was so highly organized that specialization had begun.

Herodotus, the Greek historian, observed of the Egyptians: "The art of medicine among them is distributed thus: each physician is a physician of one disease and no more . . . and the whole country is full of physicians." Some attended disorders of the eyes (ophthalmologists), others of the head (neurologists); some of the teeth (dentists), others of the bowel (gastroenterologists); and still others attended disorders perhaps less conspicuous and more general (diagnosticians). Despite such "modernity," the Egyptian pharmacopoeia included, along with good prescriptions, many that called for animal excreta, lizard's blood, swine's teeth, putrid meat and stinking fat.

Moses, knowing the limitations of the medicine of his time, rejected all of this, and formulated a concept of Public Hygiene to prevent disease. Priests were appointed public health officers, the first sanitary inspectors, and they put into effect the rules governing contagion: isolation and disinfection. The Mosaic Code covered proper food, personal hygiene, and communal health. Under it, medicinal preparations were concocted from spices and herbs, and soothing ointments from sheep fat and olive oil. Wounds were treated in the manner of the Good Samaritan, who "bound up his wounds, pouring in oil and wine" (Luke 10:34). The Hebrews' use of frankincense and myrrh, bark, aloes and cloves was superior to that of the Egyptians, many of whose weird formulas remained, however, a part of the apothecary's craft into the eighteenth century.

Moses, said de Musy, possessed "intuition prophétique des microbes." When most of the world considered disease a divine visitation or punishment, he recognized that some ills were communicable, that they could be controlled by forethought, and that contact could be reduced by isolation or quarantine.

Was it, one may wonder, a form of childbed fever that prompted Moses to consider an Israelitish woman unclean for seven days after childbearing and to exclude her from holy functions—with a group of others—for forty days? When the authorities of Venice and Marseilles suspected infection among the passengers of ships in the fourteenth century, they quarantined them for forty days. The Latin for forty is *quadraginta;* the Italian and French for forty days *quarantina* and *quarantaine*—our *quarantine*, of course. In AD 70, Titus brought to Rome from Jerusalem seventy thousand captives; they may well have introduced Moses' notion of forty days' isolation.

Moses practiced preventive, Jesus psychosomatic, medicine. "And Jesus went about all Galilee, teaching in their synagogues, and preaching the gospel of the kingdom, and healing all manner of sickness and all manner of disease among the people" (Matthew 4:23), "people that were taken with divers diseases and torments, and those which were possessed with devils, and those which were lunatick, and those that had the palsy...." Jesus knew that sickness is often the manifestation of a disturbed soul. To the man sick with palsy he said, not "Arise and walk," but, preferring to put his mind at ease, "Thy sins be forgiven thee" (Matthew 9:2).

Jesus' ministry was to the total human need. He knew what we have come to realize only recently: that much of our illness comes from broken interpersonal relations, from guilt, and from the void where no love is. His earliest doctrine linked preaching with healing: "Heal the sick, cleanse the lepers, raise the dead, cast out devils" (Matthew 10:8).

More than four centuries before Jesus, the system that became western medicine was developing under Hippocrates, "the Father of Medicine," in Greece. He set the pattern for professional attitudes and ethics, taught that observation and deduction were more important than textbook treatment, and emphasized the healing power of nature rather than of drugs. He and such giants as Aristotle, Celsus, and Dioscorides, in the following four centuries, influenced medicine for all time; but it was the great Greek physician, Galen (AD 131-200?), who modified and so perpetuated Hippocrates that he remained *the* authority for fourteen centuries, as often retarding as advancing medicine.

His father, he writes, "was amiable, just, and benevolent. My mother . . . had a very bad temper; she used to bite her serving maids, and was perpetually shouting at my father." Galen apparently inherited, writes Guthrie, the intelligence of his father, a successful architect, and the quarrelsome nature of his mother. He became physician to Emperor Marcus Aurelius Antoninus and, because of his four hundred works, the dictator of medicine.

And, as dictator, he laid a dead hand on medicine, despite

his brilliance as observer and experimentalist. Much of his philosophy—nature acted, always, with perfect wisdom; the body was "the mere vehicle for the soul"—though friendly to the Church, was inimical to the growth of medicine as a science. As late as the seventeenth century, William Harvey, author of the *Anatomical Treatise on the Movement of the Heart and Blood in Animals*, possibly the greatest book in medical literature, was bitterly attacked by the Galenists of his time and university. Countless discoveries and regimens were rejected because they were not in Galen's works, the infallible source of knowledge.

Medicine entered the long period of bondage that we call the Middle Ages, a slave to conventions that discouraged learning, experiment and originality. The Church held that nothing could detract from the Great Physician and that disease was a punishment for sin; because the body was sacred, it forbade dissection. In A.D. 391, Christian fanatics burned the great library in Alexandria and destroyed priceless treasures of learning. Yet the Church also advanced medicine, with its pity for the ill and the monks' preservation of ancient medical works.

A second great preserver of medical knowledge during the Middle Ages was Arabian medicine, so called because of the language in which the physicians wrote. Few of them were Arabs: some were Syrian, some Persian, some Spanish, and many were Christians and Jews. They approved their predecessors, translated them into Arabic, wrote commentaries on the translations, and added observations of their own, especially on epidemic fevers and diseases of the eye, common in the East. They also made large contributions in pharmacology and its ally, alchemy or chemistry.

It fell to the lot of the Jewish physician to help safeguard the medical heritage. The twelfth-century Council of Rheims interdicted the study of law and of physic to monks, and later the Lateran Council forbade physicians, under pain of exclusion from the church, to undertake medical treatment without ecclesiastical advice. So the plight of the Jewish physician in Europe of the Middle Ages was difficult. He was used and abused, a "sort of contraband luxury" resorted to by priest and prelate alike, yet hardly countenanced for any other reason. In an address on Morgagni in 1894, before the International Congress in Rome, the most famous of German pathologists, Virchow, said:

In our times Hebrew manuscripts have been brought to light which show with what zeal and learning Jewish physicians of early medieval times were active in the preservation and advancement of medicine.

The Renaissance dispelled much of the darkness of ten centuries, and gave to medical investigation a new lease on life. New and tragic diseases—syphilis, gunshot wounds—demanded attention; artists specialized in anatomy and dissection, chief amongst them Leonardo da Vinci; and Paracelsus (1493-1541) stimulated the revolt against dogmatism and roused men to seek new knowledge. He was perhaps the most original thinker of the sixteenth century: bold enough to discard Galenism, he presented the doctrine *similia similibus curantur* (like is cured by like), his "doctrine of signatures." The concept was that many diseases are cured by conditions (drugs) which produce a condition similar to the disease. In a measure, the doctrine was substantiated in 1796 when Edward Jenner, an English country doctor, introduced the practice of vaccination with cowpox for the prevention of smallpox. And in our own day, the use of typhoid and live "polio" virus vaccines, as well as the treatment of non-contagious disorders such as hay fever and allergies by minute but increasing doses of the offending pollen or allergen, is in consonance with the principle of *similia similibus curantur*.

The great medical leaders of the sixteenth century—Paracelsus, Paré, and Vesalius, the latter famed for the accuracy of his anatomical descriptions—blazed the way for the general advance of medicine to follow. Other notables of the era were the Spaniard, Michael Servetus, who first described the pulmonary circulation (1553), and the Englishman, William Harvey (1578-1657), who discovered the circulation of the blood and founded modern physiology.

Specialization was not completely resurrected until recent times, although given impetus by the Royal College of Physicians (formed under the guidance of a physician-priest, Thomas Linacre, in 1518), which regulated a physician's work and encouraged interest in particular fields of medicine. Notwithstanding the contributions of individual men throughout the Renaissance, witness the condition of medicine in England during the seventeenth century as recorded by Dr. Gideon Harvey. He classified the physicians into six sects: one, chalybeate doctors, who cured all diseases with preparations of steel or copper (much like the modern physicians who give iron and vitamins with minerals to all patients); two, medical ass-drivers, who put all their patients on diets of asses' milk (to this day, a diet of goat's milk is not infrequently prescribed); three, jesuitical doctors, who depended upon bark (quinine, originally obtained from Peruvian tree bark, is often used to differentiate malarial fever from other febrile illnesses); four, water bailiffs, who drenched their patients at the mineral springs (spas are still popular today); five, butcher doctors, who always bled their patients (some surgeons, afflicted with "furor operativa," still do); and six, illustrious muck doctors, who expelled diseases by purgation (calomel is still used). Has the old order changed or do we now simply have a new set of categories: vitamin pill pushers, antibiotic enthusiasts, hormone hustlers, appendix apprehenders, mammary misogynists, dilation and curettage deceivers, uterine usurpers—hewers of flesh and drawers of water?

The physician of three hundred years ago was permitted to practice both medicine and surgery; his colleague, the surgeon—a man with certain mechanical or technical skills —was allowed only to perform surgery and not to presume to treat medical ailments. He was called not *Doctor* but *Mister,* which the surgeon in Great Britain, disdaining the generally more honored title, retains. Today, the order is reversed. The specialist in internal medicine may practice medicine but not surgery; the surgeon, on the other hand, performs surgery and often practices a great deal of medicine besides.

A bit of insight into the state of medical affairs in England early in the eighteenth century—when crab's-eye powder was still a medicament—may be gleaned from the quarrel between Bidloo, the Dutch doctor who was brought to England from the famed University of Leyden by King William III to serve as his personal physician, and Ronjat, the French surgeon who was also in the king's entourage. The king had fallen from his horse during the hunt, and his shoulder bone was believed to be broken. Bidloo wanted to put on the bandages but Ronjat objected vehemently, saying "C'est moi qui suis le premier chirurgien du Roi" (It is I who am the first surgeon to the King).

Though the Royal Society had spread the news of the amazing discoveries that were taking place, nevertheless there was much resistance to the progress that experimental methods had made possible. In such an atmosphere, there was no place for Harvey's *De Motu Cordis,* since Hippocrates, Galen and Avicenna had said nothing about circulation of the blood. As for Paracelsus, his name was blasphemy. In France, for instance, the Paris faculty zealously guarded their rights and privileges against all interlopers: apothecaries and barber-surgeons were classed as vile conspirators against the medical profession. Blood letting and purgation were the typical approach of the day; though Harvey and his successors had proved them nonsense, their use died slowly. Polypharmacy—prescriptions contained dozens of ingredients, including live worms, vipers' flesh, and bezoar stones—flourished. Guy Patin, spokesman of the Paris school at mid-seventeenth century, rightfully preached a return to simple remedies, and fought against the encroachments of new-fangled medicines, particularly the use of antimony. Incidentally, Patin also opposed the barber-surgeons since they, too, were trying to usurp the province of the academicians, but, thanks to a fistula in the royal anus (an ailment of Louis XIV), the surgeons soon moved up in status.

The petty jealousies that stigmatized French medicine gradually disappeared, and the nineteenth century ushered in a new era for France. Thanks to Napoleon's patronage, abundant facilities were provided for hospital care and, fortunately, the medical talent was ready: Paris became, for a time, the scientific capital of the world. The first stethoscope—today's symbol of the doctor—was invented by Réné-Théophile Laennec in 1816, and every physician who listens to the chest with this instrument will ever remain in his debt. The blessing of the nineteenth century was the uniting of science with medicine, a fact which Lord Lister of *asepsis* fame movingly pointed out in his memorable address on December 27, 1892, at the Sorbonne in Paris, when Louis Pasteur was honored by the world on the occasion of his seventieth birthday.

The modern "father of medicine," Sir William Osler—a product of the nineteenth century—said this of his times:

"To us in the medical profession . . . whose work is with the sick and suffering, the great boon of this wonderful century . . . is the fact that the leaves of the tree of Science have been for the healing of nations. This is the Promethean gift of the century to man."

It is the twentieth century, however, that has witnessed the greatest achievements in the biologic sciences. The technologic and scientific advances in medicine have been greater in the past fifty years than in all the years of our civilization. A prerequisite for our modern technical development is a very high degree of specialization: the necessity of subdividing knowledge as it expands has forced the creation of specialties and subspecialties.

Specialization in the medical arts proceeds at a fast pace today. Internal medicine is divided into a dozen or more specialties: allergy, dermatology, cardiology, gastroenterology, endocrinology, and peripheral hematology. Surgery has gone just as far, with its abdominal, thoracic, gynecologic, urologic, vascular, plastic, and neurologic surgeons, among others. No one will deny that all this indicates some sort of progress, but the boundary between one surgical specialty and another is frequently difficult to define. The urethra, the vagina, and the rectum occupy so circumscribed an area that, literally, a fine line demarcates the province of the urologist, the gynecologist, and the proctologist. One slip, and where is the surgeon?—in another's territory.

The human side of medicine has changed. Better educated and informed—often enough misinformed, also, by television, comic strips, and "feature articles"—the public knows more about diseases and their treatments, and the impact of science and social change has altered the patient's attitude toward his doctor. The patient has lost his awe, perhaps, of the physician, often divesting himself of the faith that also cures, especially in functional illness, and building within himself false images.

It would be folly to ignore the fact that the medical profession has lost face in our society. The image of the selfless, dedicated physician has been beclouded. But why? Is it that the "bedside manner" has disappeared because new diagnostic laboratory tests, specific drugs, technical equipment, and surgical skills have contributed to a change from a warm friendly relationship to one colder, more calculated, less personal—and that, although medical care is better by far than ever before, the medical profession has deteriorated in the public eye?

The mortality of acute pneumonia has been reduced from twenty-five per cent and more to one per cent and, frequently, all that is required of the patient is to swallow eight pills a day. In a former day, the physician labored for days, keeping a fearful vigil with the family as the patient approached a successful crisis, or his demise. The family physician then had few tools, but he offered warmth, comfort and his unhurried attentions; today he has too often appeared to be a cold, calculating instrument of science. The emotional disenchantment between patient and physician started with the vanishing family doctor and the emergence of the specialist. Depth of personal understanding has yielded to breadth of medical knowledge.

Perhaps the objective methodology inherited from Hippocratic medicine of yesteryear and the impersonal precision and efficiency of present-day specialists are not enough. Sympathy and love identified with the healing acts of Jesus, and the concern for the healthy individual as the unit of communal welfare, as bequeathed to us by Moses, are ingredients that are missing in the prescriptions for the ills of mankind.

As the panorama of the healing art unfolds, one cannot fail to be impressed by the changing image of the healer. The need for the physician ever increases, for the sick will always be with us. In spite of the progress made in the last century, the physically ill and the mentally distraught fill our hospitals to overflowing, and one is constrained to ask with Jeremiah (8:22):

Is there no balm in Gilead; is there no physician there? why then is not the health of the daughter of my people recovered?

Search the Scriptures

The Oath of Hippocrates has traditionally served as the standard for ethical practice, but no more beautiful guide may be found than the lesser known *Oath and Prayer of Moses Maimonides,* twelfth-century physician. This reads, in part:

> O, grant—
> That neither greed for gain, nor thirst for fame,
>   nor vain ambition,
> May interfere with my activity.
> For these I know are enemies of truth and love
>   of men,
> And might beguile one in my profession
> From furthering the welfare of Thy creatures.
> O strengthen me.
> Grant energy unto both body and the soul
> That I might e'er unhindered ready be
> To mitigate the woes,
> Sustain and help
> The rich and poor, the good and bad, enemy
>   and friend.
> O let me e'er behold in the afflicted and suffering,
> Only the human being.

GLOSSARY

ACHONDROPLASTIC. Affected with ACHONDROPLASIA, imperfect ossification within the long bones, producing dwarfism.
ADRENALIN. Proprietary brand of EPINEPHRINE, a drug that increases cardiac output and constricts peripheral blood vessels.
ANABOLIC. Pertaining to ANABOLISM, constructive metabolism, the assimilation of nutritive matter and conservation of proteins. CATABOLISM is destructive metabolism.
ANDROGEN. Hormone that increases maleness.
ANEMIA. A condition in which the red corpuscles of the blood are reduced in number or are deficient in hemoglobin.
ANOREXIA. Loss of appetite.
AUTONOMIC NERVOUS SYSTEM. A part of the nervous system that controls involuntary bodily functions.
AUTOSOMES. Any ordinary chromosomes as distinguished from sex chromosomes. See CHROMOSOMES.
BALANITIS. Inflammation of the glans penis.
CARBOHYDRATES. Sugar, starches, celluloses, gums.
CATABOLIC. See ANABOLIC.
CHROMOSOME COMPLEX. The normal 22 pairs of autosomes plus 1 pair of sex chromosomes, totaling 46.
CHROMOSOMES. Bodies present in nuclei of cells of all species that carry hereditary factors.
CIRCULATORY FAILURE. Failure of system to deliver sufficient blood to the tissues for their metabolic needs.
CORNIFICATION. Superficial protective covering of skin composed of keratin or horny substance.
CORONA. Prominent posterior border of the glans penis.
DERMATITIS. Inflatmmation of the skin.
DIGITALIS. The dried leaves of the foxglove plant used as a cardiac tonic and diuretic.
ENDROCRINE GLANDS. Glands that produce secretions (hormones) that pass directly into the blood stream and affect body functions.
EPIDEMIOLOGY. The science of epidemics and epidemic diseases.
EPINEPHRINE. See ADRENALIN.
EUNUCH. One whose testicles have been removed or, if present, are non-functional.
EUPHORIA. The state of wellbeing.

EXOPHTHALMIC GOITER. A condition characterized by protrusion of the eyeballs in association with an overactive thyroid gland.
GLANS. The tissue comprising the head of the penis.
GYNECOLOGIC. Pertaining to women's diseases.
HEMOLYSIS. Destruction of red blood cells.
HERMAPHRODITE. A person with both male and female generative organs.
HYPERESTHESIA. Excessive sensitivity to touch.
HYPOTHYROIDISM. A condition due to deficiency of the thyroid hormone.
IATROGENIC. Induced by a physician: a term applied to disorders resulting from the activity of physicians.
INSULIN. The hormone secreted by the pancreas that helps in the utilization of blood sugar.
KLINEFELTER'S SYNDROME. A condition in the adult male characterized by breast enlargement and small testicles.
LIBIDO. Conscious or unconscious sexual drive.
MENARCHE. The establishment of the menstrual function.
MENOPAUSE. Permanent cessation of the menses.
NYMPHOMANIA. Excessive and frenetic sexual desire in the female.
ORTHOPEDIC. Pertaining to disorders of bones and joints.
OVARIAN. Concerning or resembling the ovary.
OVULATION. The process of discharging the ovum (egg) from the ovary.
PATHOGENESIS. Mode of origin or development of any disease or morbid process.
PHALLUS. The penis.
PHIMOSIS. Narrowness of the opening of the prepuce preventing its being drawn back over the glans.
PITUITARY GLAND. A small gland, attached to the base of the brain, that secretes a number of hormones that regulate many bodily processes.
POTENTIA. Ability to perform sexual intercourse.
PREPUCE. Foreskin of penis.
PROGESTERONE. A hormone secreted by the ovary and placenta for preparation and maintenance of pregnancy.
PROTEINS. A class of nitrogenous compounds; an essential component of all living matter, animal or vegetable.
PUBERTY-PUBESCENCE. The age at which the reproductive organs become functionally operative and secondary sexual characteristics develop.
PSYCHONEUROSIS. Neurosis based on conflict in which some impulse has been blocked and seeks expression in some disguised response or symptom.
SEMINAL. Relating to the fluid produced by the male generative organs.
SERPASIL. Proprietary brand of RESERPINE, a tranquilizing agent.

Glossary

TESTICULAR. Pertaining to the testes (the male gonads).

TESTOSTERONE. The principal masculinizing hormone.

TRANSVESTISM. The practice of masquerading in the clothes of the opposite sex.

TURNER'S SYNDROME. A condition characterized by short stature and sexual infantilism associated with failure of the ovaries to develop beyond the rudimentary stage.

UTERINE. Relating to the womb (the uterus).

VIRILITY. Manliness.

INDEX OF NAMES

Abishag, 139, 142
Abraham, 58-59, 84, 113-115
Absalom, 7
Adam, 105, 125
Aesculapius, 80
Antiochus, 64
Aristotle, 54, 152
Astarte, 120
Attila, 43
Augustine, 56
Avicenna, 156

Banks, Dr. Lawrence, 31
Banting, Sir Frederick Grant, 68
Bath-Sheba, 139, 141
Beauvoir, Simone de—*The Second Sex,* 117
Beethoven, Ludwig van, 43-44
Benedict, Dr. Stanley R., 100
Bernard, Claude, 52
Berossos, 144
Berthold of Göttingen, 55
Bidloo, Govert, 156
Bilhah, 29
Bloom, Dr. Walter, 100
Bogen, Emil, 94
Browning, Robert—"Rabbi Ben Ezra," 117
Brown-Sequard, Charles-Edouard, 52-53
Byron, George Gordon—*Childe Harold,* 44

Caffarelli, Gaetano, 56
Cannon, Walter B., 100
Carnera, Primo, 41
Castor, 33
Celsus, 152

Charles II, 134
Chaucer, Geoffrey—*Canterbury Tales,* Pardoner, 53-54
  Physician, 13
Churchill, W., 62
Crooke, Dr. C. A., 35

Daniel, 98
Darwin, Erasmus, 80
David, 7, 11, 37-41, 82, 84, 138-140, 143
da Vinci, Leonardo, 154
Delilah, 17, 19-20
Dempsey, Jack, 41
d'Éon, Chevalier, 119
Dioscorides, 29-30, 109, 152
Dock, Dr. William, 96
Donini, Dr. Pietro, 34
Donne, John—"Song," 30
Driver, S. R., 60
Dumas, A., *Le Vicomte de Bragellone,* 34
Duncan, Dr. Garfield, 100

Ecclesiastes, 143, 150
Eddruff, Rev. E. P., 132
Edward the Confessor, 134
Ellis, Havelock, 119
Esau, 9, 33, 67-71
Eve, 125, 133

Farinelli, Carlo, 56
Firpo, Luis, 41
Fosdick, Harry Emerson, 106
Franco, Francisco, 43
Freud, Sigmund, 48, 118

Galen, 108, 152, 153, 156

165

Gandhi, Mahatma, 99, 101, 109
Gardner, John, 109
Garrison, Dr. Fielding Hudson, 14
Gellius, Aulus, 132
Gemzell, Dr. Carl, 35
Goering, H., 61
Goldberg, Dr. Minnie B., 116
Goldburg, Rev. Dr. Norman, 14, 112
Goliath, 11, 37-41, 140
Guthrie, Dr. Douglas—*A History of Medicine*, 152

Hagar, 115
Hamburger, Dr. Christian, 121-122
Handel, Georg Friedrich, *Samson*, 19-20
Harris, Dr. Seale, 68, 69
Harvey, Dr. Gideon, 158
Harvey, William, 153, 155
Hawthorne, Nathaniel—*The Scarlet Letter*, 124
Hendry, Charles, 27
Hercules, "infant," 70
Hermaphroditus, 105
Herodotus, 150
Hippocrates, 80, 109, 152, 156, 160
Hirschfeld, Dr. Magnus, 119
Hitler, Adolf, 26, 43
Hogarth, William, 110
Hosea, 92
Huggins, Dr. Charles, 55

Isaac, 67
Isaiah, 92, 124, 126, 128

Jacob, 28, 32, 33, 48, 67-71
James, 77
Jarvis, Dr. D. C., *Folk Medicine*, 110, 111
Jenner, Edward, 154
Jeremiah, 159
Jesus, and circumcision, 64; eunuchs, 51, 54, 56-57; fasting, 98; genealogy, 84; healing, 135, 151-152, 159; Magdalene, 20-21; sacrifice, 126; vinegar, 111-112; wine, 89; Zaccheus, 42-43.
Job, 7
John the Baptist, 64
Johnson, Dr. Samuel, on wine and drinking, 96
Joseph, 47-50, 64
Josephus, 57
Josiah, 121
Judah, 18, 33, 120

Kinsey, Alfred, 120
Koheleth, 144, 145

Laban, 28, 32
Laennec, Réné-Théophile, 157
Lazarus, Emma, 26
Leah, 28-29, 30
Leo XIII, Pope, 56
Linacre, Thomas, 155
Lister, Joseph, Baron Lister, 157
Loeb, Dr. Jacques, 74
Longfellow, Henry Wadsworth—"Morituri Salutamus," 147-148
Lot, daughters, 90
Luce, Claire B., 24
Lucia, Dr. Salvatore P.—*A History of Wine As Therapy*, 90, 96
Luke the Physician, 134, 151
Lunenfeld, Dr. Bruno, 34

MacSwiney, Terence, 99-100, 101
Maimonides, Rabbi Moses ben Maimon, 160
Marie, Pierre, 39
Mark, 111
Marriott, Dr. H. L., 74
Martel, Charles, 72
Mary Magdalene, 17, 20
Matthew, 51, 54, 56, 89, 111
Methusaleh, 143
Milton, John—
Paradise Regained, 123

Index of Names

Paradise Lost, 80, 126
Samson Agonistes, 19
Montagu, Ashley, 131
Moses, 39, 76, 86, 98, 118, 143, 151, 159
Mussolini, Benito, 43

Napoleon Bonaparte, 43-44, 72, 157
Niebuhr, R., 27
Noah, 90

Onan, 22
Osler, Sir William, 7, 157

Paracelsus, 154, 156
Pardoner, Chaucer's, 53-54
Paré, Ambroise, 31, 154
Pasteur, Louis, 89, 157
Patin, Guy, 156
Paul, 11, 23, 24, 65, 72-77, 85, 88, 92, 96
Peter, 77
Pharaoh, 49
Pharez, 33
Philip III, of Spain, 43
Pick, Dr. Alois, 90
Pilate, Pontius, 111
Pollux, 33
Pope, Pius XI, 23
Pope, Pius XII, 24
Potiphar, 47, 49
Potiphar's wife, 47-48
Powers, John J., 90
Proverbs, on wine, 91, 92-93, 131

Rachel, 28-29, 30, 31
Ramadan, fast of, 99
Rebekah, 67, 70
Reimann, Dr. Hobart A., 86
Remus, 33
Reuben, 28-29
Rolfe, Gov. James, Jr., 112
Romulus, 33
Ronjat, 156
Rothschild, 78
Rubens, Peter Paul, 126
Ruth, 108-109

Saint-Saens, Charles Camillo—
 Samson et Dalila, 20
Samson, 19-20
Samuel, 141
Sarah, 113-115
Saul, 37-41, 45, 72-77, 140
Saul of Tarsus, 11
Selvinov, 56
Selye, Dr. Hans, 105
Servetus, Michael, 106, 155
Shakespeare, William—
 Anthony and Cleopatra, 30
 As You Like It, 144
 Hamlet, 103-104
 II Henry IV, 147
 Julius Caesar, 101
 King Lear, 136
 Macbeth, 94, 115-116
 Merchant of Venice, 32
 Othello, 30
 Romeo and Juliet, 29
 The Comedy of Errors, 144
 The Rape of Lucrece, 81
 The Winter's Tale, 69
Sherman, Dr. David, 148
Skoptsi, 56
Smith, Homer, 102
Snively, Dr. W. D., Jr., 75
Socrates, 129
Solomon, 84, 86, 129-130, 132, 139
Stevenson, Robert Louis, 14

Talmud, 94
Tamar, 17, 18, 22, 33
Tennyson, Alfred, Lord—
 "Ulysses," 44, 148, 149
 "The Passing of Arthur," from the Idylls of the King, 103
Thomas, 33
Timothy, 88
Titian, Vecelli, 126
Titus, 151
Toulouse-Lautrec, Henri Marie Raymond, 43
Tyler, Dr. Edward, 24

Uriah, 141

Vague, Dr. Jean, 121
Valesii, 56
Veilluti, 56
Vesalius, Andreas, 154
Virchow, Rudolf, 154
Viterbi, 99

Washington, George, 62
"Wicked woman" of Proverbs, 17, 19
Wordsworth, William—
"My Heart Leaps Up," 123

Zaccheus, 42-46
Zarah, 33
Zilpah, 29